CHINA's
COSMOLOGICAL
PREHISTORY

"Yet another important piece to Scranton's ongoing quest to prove that a near identical cosmology was common knowledge around the entire globe in ancient prehistory. Perhaps the 'single language' posited in the Book of Genesis, the 'language' that once 'united all mankind,' was not mere fabrication and/or wishful thinking after all. It was cosmology as Scranton again demonstrates."

JOHN ANTHONY WEST,
AUTHOR OF *SERPENT IN THE SKY:
THE HIGH WISDOM OF ANCIENT EGYPT*

"Laird Scranton's research into cosmological historical frameworks is profound, diligent, and meticulous. Not only does he unveil the underpinnings of significant lexicons and high science, but he reveals how they weave synchronicities and commonalities across unexpected demographics in a pioneering way. The sensational revelation is at the very least a common original source. In *China's Cosmological Prehistory* another awe-inspiring wealth of realization is brought to the forefront with an academic style and unique perspective. Undoubtedly, the importance of Scranton's continued work and research in this book and previous works will be revered by future generations of researchers."

E. A. JAMES SWAGGER,
AUTHOR OF *THE NEWGRANGE SIRIUS MYSTERY:
LINKING PASSAGE GRAVE COSMOLOGY WITH DOGON SYMBOLOGY*

CHINA'S COSMOLOGICAL PREHISTORY

The Sophisticated Science Encoded
in Civilization's Earliest Symbols

LAIRD SCRANTON

Inner Traditions
Rochester, Vermont • Toronto, Canada

Inner Traditions
One Park Street
Rochester, Vermont 05767
www.InnerTraditions.com

SUSTAINABLE FORESTRY INITIATIVE Certified Sourcing
www.sfiprogram.org
SFI-00854

Text stock is SFI certified

Library of Congress Cataloging-in-Publication Data

Scranton, Laird, 1953–
  China's cosmological prehistory : the sophisticated science encoded in
civilization's earliest symbols / Laird Scranton.
    pages cm
    Includes bibliographical references and index.
    ISBN 978-1-62055-329-9 (paperback) — ISBN 978-1-62055-330-5 (e-book)
  1. Cosmology, Chinese. I. Title.
    BD518.C5S37 2014
    113.0931—dc23

                                                                    2014005704

Printed and bound in the United States by Lake Book Manufacturing, Inc.
The text stock is SFI certified. The Sustainable Forestry Initiative® program
promotes sustainable forest management.

10 9 8 7 6 5 4 3 2 1

Text design and layout by Virginia L. Scott Bowman
This book was typeset in Garamond Premier Pro with Trajan Pro used as the
display typeface

To send correspondence to the author of this book, mail a first-class letter to the
author c/o Inner Traditions • Bear & Company, One Park Street, Rochester, VT
05767, and we will forward the communication, or contact the author directly at
http://lairdscranton.com.

CONTENTS

ACKNOWLEDGMENTS

The impulse to write this book has come largely as the result of the encouragement of others. In particular I want to thank John Anthony West for his ongoing interest, support, and belief in the work I do. I greatly appreciate the many opportunities and doors opened to me by Walter Cruttenden. I also want to thank Rhoda Lerman for her enthusiastic, generous, and always insightful support of my work. Likewise, this book would not have been possible without the proactive friendship and investigative efforts of Ed Nightingale, whose many insights into the secrets of the Giza Plateau catalyzed much of the research that spawned this book. I want to thank Argentinian filmmaker Pablo Cesar for his talent, enthusiasm, dedication, and steadfast belief in my work. I also owe a great debt of thanks to my dear wife Risa and our two remarkable offspring, Isaac and Hannah, who have always been my unwavering supporters. I also want to acknowledge the friends and family who often serve as sounding boards for the range of sometimes outrageous ideas I explore, including my brother David Scranton and longtime friends Will Newman, Sue Clark, Tom Herlihy, and Nilifur Clubwala. Finally, I owe a great debt to the late Walter Fairservis, the Vassar College professor of anthropology, whose courses I never actually took, but whose work laid an important foundation for several pivotal concepts developed in this book.

INTRODUCTION

This is the fourth in a series of books about the creation traditions (or cosmologies) of ancient cultures. The purpose of these books is to discuss the underlying foundations of ancient cosmology and language, and to explore the many commonalities that are evident among classic ancient creation traditions. The series began with *The Science of the Dogon,* a work that examines the intriguing system of myths and symbols of a modern-day African tribe from Mali called the Dogon and the many parallels it exhibits, both to the creation traditions of various ancient cultures and to modern cosmological science. These initial discussions continued in a second volume titled *Sacred Symbols of the Dogon,* in which I outlined an alternate approach to interpreting ancient Egyptian hieroglyphic symbols and words, using Dogon cosmological terms and drawings as a reference. In the third and most recent book of the series, *The Cosmological Origins of Myth and Symbol,* I correlated aspects of the Dogon and Egyptian cosmologies to the very similar ancient Buddhist stupa tradition in India. I also compiled a list of attributes that are commonly shared by the Dogon, Egyptian, and Buddhist cosmologies, which proved to be predictive of what I found as I examined the outwardly similar creation tradition and hieroglyphic language of a little-known Tibetan and Chinese culture called the Na-khi (whose name is sometimes given as Na-xi).

The Dongba language of the Na-khi is the last known surviving hieroglyphic language in the world and is considered to have been a predecessor to the Chinese hieroglyphic language. It is also believed that this written language was primarily intended to express concepts of cosmology, since the set of glyphs it defines are not capable of expressing the full spectrum of ideas that relate to the daily life of the Na-khi. So both the cosmology and the associated hieroglyphic language of the Na-khi suggested that ancient creation traditions in China could be fundamentally similar to the ones I was already pursuing. I also knew that the earliest cosmological references in China date from around the same period as similar references in ancient Egypt, as does the approximate time frame for the emergence of written Chinese language. So since my intention has been to sustain a coherent cosmological and geographical progression for our studies, it made sense that China would become the focus of this latest book in my series.

From many different perspectives, China has long been an enigma to Western cultures, so it should come as no surprise that ancient Chinese religious traditions and practices often reflect similarly enigmatic aspects. Some of the mystery of these traditions may reflect tangible differences in mind-sets between Eastern and Western cultures; some of it may be the result of the long periods of relative isolation that have existed in China that have shielded some of these traditions from outside view. Some may be the result of modern political trends that work to de-emphasize ancestral religious traditions in China. However, it may also be possible that some of these mysteries of Eastern thought simply coincide with obscure aspects of the ancient esoteric tradition that I have been working to decipher.

In this current volume, my approach to exploring the ancient Chinese creation tradition will take a form similar to the method I employed when studying the Na-khi. It is my intention to revisit each of the points of the civilizing plan outlined in *The Cosmological Origins of Myth and Symbol* and discuss how they may or may not have applied to ancient China. I plan to consider how Chinese concepts of cosmology were expressed in various myths, symbols, words, and concepts. Through these discussions I hope to gain new insights about shared aspects of the Dogon, Egyptian, and Buddhist cosmologies and to test the limits of possible correspondence to ancient Chinese traditions. I intend to discuss important themes of ancient Chinese cosmology that may not have played a well-defined role in the traditions of the other cultures I have studied. It is also my purpose to consider Chinese perspectives on various themes of cosmology and language already introduced in prior volumes of this series.

In the case of ancient China, as we will explore together in the following pages, we may find that there is less direct evidence on which to base our observations than in other cultures I have studied. This circumstance arises largely because events that transpired in China in the era of 3000 BCE were often not reflected in surviving written texts until many centuries later. Consequently, we find less consensus of opinion among scholars as to the true nature of any particular aspect of cosmology in earliest China.[1] Sarah Allan writes in *The Shape of the Turtle: Myth, Art, and Cosmos in Early China:*

> One problem in reconstruction is that there are very few texts from the period immediately following the overthrow of the Shang. Indeed, it is some five centuries before we begin to have a significant corpus of literature. Another problem is that early Chinese texts do not normally recount myth, even euhemerized as history, except in very abbreviated references within the context of other discussion. These references must be pieced together to form an intelligible pattern.[2]

The lack of scholarly consensus can mean that definitions comparable to ones that are often overtly stated among the Dogon and the Buddhists, or that may be broadly agreed on by most traditional Egyptologists, may seem to be "carved in mud" rather than stone when it comes to ancient China. In China, fundamental disagreements can

persist over even the most rudimentary aspects of historical or cosmological study, such as to which specific group of deities a traditional
title may refer or whether a given term properly represents the name
of a deity or the name of a dynasty. Even in situations where a single
opinion may predominate, there often remains a significant amount of
"wiggle room" when it comes to any finalized definition. Consequently,
it becomes difficult to make definitive statements with any degree of
confidence. For a researcher such as myself, whose preference it is to
frame each interpretation in relation to an overt statement on the part
of the culture involved, the only secure interpretation is one that can be
effectively anchored in some tangible way. The difficulty of doing this
in relation to ancient China may require us to find novel approaches to
validating our interpretations in this study.

My view of ancient cosmology as an instructed plan implies, in
regard to its study in China and in other cultures, that any such plan
would have existed in its most coherent form at the time when it was
initially presented. This means that, for the sake of our comparative
studies, we will want to focus our attention on the very earliest forms
in each culture. If these systems were initially similar to one another,
then it makes sense that changes introduced over time could be largely
responsible for the divergences we will see in the surviving elements of
the various traditions we will compare. From that standpoint, it makes
sense that we assign less weight to how cultures interpreted these symbolic elements at 300 BCE than we might to how the same elements are
understood to have existed at 3000 BCE. We should understand that
these exercises in comparative cosmology would not likely be fruitful
unless the creation traditions of the cultures involved were at one time
fundamentally similar to one another; otherwise, our studies would
simply amount to comparing apples to oranges, and so would reveal
only the occasional or random similarity. The greater the number of
parallels we are able to credibly demonstrate between the cosmologies of
these cultures, the more sensible our argument becomes that they were
all once fundamentally similar.

Historically, ancient China was home to a number of outwardly different religious traditions, although an overlap in concepts and practices among those traditions can often be seen. It is firmly documented that in the late centuries BCE or early centuries CE, a wide variety of religious doctrines were introduced into ancient China, although only a few of these ultimately took root. For example, Buddhist practices are known to have been brought to China from India and to have greatly influenced the religious profiles of China and Japan. One question that scholars still ponder centers on why Buddhism came to be so warmly embraced in China, when other traditions apparently were not. Any early links we may uncover in China to a shared plan of cosmology could argue that the archaic Chinese traditions had originally been framed in similar ways to the ancient Vedic tradition in India.

Written language also went through a series of transitions in China, so our best hope for positive correlation to other writing systems may again lie with its earliest forms. However, there are certain outward features of Chinese language that we can immediately see align well with what we know to be true about the Egyptian hieroglyphs. First, each Chinese glyph or character is understood to represent a tangible concept, object, or action. Therefore, the process of reading a Chinese word involves a process similar to what I have employed for ancient Egyptian hieroglyphic words: substituting concepts for glyphs to create a kind of symbolic sentence, rather than replacing letters with phonetic values, as is the practice in many modern languages. Like the Egyptian hieroglyphic language, Chinese writing encompasses literally thousands of different glyphs. Just as the spoken language of the Dogon combines a number of simple, predefined phonemes to create more complex words, so a Chinese glyph can sometimes be formed by combining a series of discrete signs, each with its own associated meaning. And like the Egyptian glyphs, any given Chinese glyph may convey more than one symbolic meaning.

When working with any single one of these ancient creation traditions, it is not uncommon to discover a theme or reference that is not well defined or that does not seem to connect in a meaningful way with what I have seen in other cultures, so it constitutes a kind of symbolic loose end. This can leave us with unresolved questions about how and why the reference might have come to exist and how it properly relates to a larger system of references. Each time we examine the similar creation tradition of another culture, evidence can turn up to resolve some of these loose ends. The same is often true in regard to the meanings of certain less-well-understood symbols. For example, it sometimes will become clear from our readings of Egyptian words that a certain glyph shape must imply a particular symbolic concept. However, even though the meaning is implied contextually, it might not always be clear why the concept pertains to that specific symbol. As we expand our base of referent cultures, languages, and creation traditions, a more multi-dimensional picture begins to emerge and we sometimes find that an underlying rationale for these symbolic assignments becomes evident.

Many of the interpretations I will put forth in this volume regarding symbols and their likely meanings will be based on resemblances that can be shown to exist between cosmological words. One of the China scholars whose work I rely on as a reference for Chinese cosmology, Norman J. Girardot, flatly rejects this method of interpretation. His view is that to base an inference about Chinese symbolism on the similar pronunciation of two words would be as meaningless as trying to pose an argument about modern word meanings based on the idea that the word *egg* sounds like the word *keg*.[3] However, it is a clearly stated principle among the Dogon and the Egyptian priests that similarities of pronunciation imply a conceptual relationship between two words. Also, in my view, the key terms of ancient cosmology, unlike ordinary words in everyday usage, constitute a very special case because they relate to what is apparently an organized system. If it can be convincingly shown that other aspects of this system existed in similar form in ancient China, then the validity of this same principle of pronunciation is arguably implied there.

Our ability to favorably compare the meanings of cosmological terms from different cultures is one way of demonstrating that the cosmologies were fundamentally similar. Differences in the nuances of meaning that may exist between these words can often shed new light on the cosmological concept that is actually being expressed. When the words are also defined in relation to the same mythic theme or symbol in both cultures, then these references provide us with further means to cross-check and confirm the likely meanings of the shared terms. It is enormously helpful to my studies that the authors of many of my source references take special care to explain the many shades of meaning that may attach to these words. This practice reflects a well-founded understanding on the part of these authors that such references may prove invaluable to other researchers.

Numbers also play a significant role in aligning the traditions of various cultures—both the recurrence of certain key numbers themselves and the specific symbolism associated with those numbers. Some of these, such as the number of days in a year, were simply dictated by nature. However, others reflect a consistency of practice from culture to culture that has no obvious root in environment. For example, it seems curious that the Chinese and Egyptians both chose matching units of measure for time (a 360-day year, 30-day month, 10-day week, 24-hour day, and 60-minute hour) that appear to have been founded on even factors of the grand cycle of precession (the very gradual apparent rotation of the background constellations in relation to the rising sun).

The success that I have met with so far in these cross-cultural comparisons outlines important ways in which many ancient creation traditions seem remarkably similar to one another. For example, anthropologists know that ancestor worship was a common feature of ancient cultures, but they may not always be aware that this reverence for ancestors was often expressed in markedly similar ways from culture to culture. For example, it may be a natural human instinct to honor the memory of your predecessors. However, there is nothing in that impulse to insist that these predecessors be conceptualized as seven ancestors or in relation to seven honored ancestral families. Yet we can see this same organizational framework for the notion of ancestors, expressed in similar terms, in culture after ancient culture. Likewise, because mothers are pivotal to a familial society, it seems natural that cultures would evolve traditions that honor a mother goddess. It may even seem natural to associate the mother as a giver of life with the formation of matter. But nowhere in that mind-set do we find natural associations with the concepts of waves, weaving, and spirals that predominate so many ancient concepts of how matter is formed. The suggestion is that some factor other than mere human impulse could be at work here.

As I have worked with these ancient traditions, one thing I have noticed is that the same subtle rules of symbolism apply to each system that I explore. During the early, noniconic periods of each tradition, I can see that animals became associated with concepts. Owls came to symbolize knowledge and elephants came to imply abundance. Eventually serpents, which were initially revered, came to represent evil. In later periods, deities took on associations with specific animals. Oftentimes the symbolism assigned to an animal reflected some salient aspect of that creature; for example, in Dogon culture, the twitching of a rabbit or hare came to represent the concept of vibration. By the historic era, starting with the earliest surviving written text from around 2600 BCE, the rulers of many cultures (often cast as representatives of gods) had adopted much of the same animal symbolism that had been initially assigned to deities. Not only did various rules of symbolism seem to cross the boundaries of sometimes distant cultures, but so did the evolutionary trends of association and occasional outright reversals of that symbolism. Again, we can see some cross-cultural force at play other than natural human tendencies.

A number of different theories have been put forth to explain the near-universal nature of various themes and symbols of the ancient creation traditions. Perhaps cultures that are at the same stage of development simply tend to create similar forms. Or perhaps humanity is psychologically "wired" to conceptualize themes of creation in specific ways. My outlook is that the complex symbolism that attaches to various cosmological forms flatly contradicts any theory of parallel development, especially when that symbolism seems logically distanced from the form itself. In China, we find a set of traditions that were for many years also geographically and culturally distanced from the other ancient traditions. Surely if we were looking for a unique set of ancient practices, we would expect to find them in a location as remote as China. However, given the many commonalities known to have existed among the cosmological traditions of ancient Africa, Egypt, India, and Asia, the coincidence of finding many of these same elements in China could argue convincingly that in ancient times, the common system of creation I propose for these cultures also exerted a contemporaneous influence in ancient China.

In the course of this book, I will of necessity draw on concepts and background from the three earlier books in my series on creation traditions and cosmologies. I will, however, endeavor to include enough information so that you will be able to enjoy this book fully without having read the others. Of course, if you want to know more, they are there for you to delve into (if you have not already). For now, let us embark on our journey to ancient China together.

1
CONTOURS OF A SHARED CREATION TRADITION

My comparative studies in cosmology began with an obscure African tribe from Mali (located in the "hump" of northwest Africa) called the Dogon. Since much of the comparative information we will rely on for our study of China comes from the Dogon, it makes sense before we begin these comparisons to summarize a few important aspects of their culture and cosmology. This modern-day primitive tribe, which consists of around three hundred thousand individuals, makes an excellent starting point for our comparisons because their society centers on aspects of several different classic ancient traditions. For example, Dogon ritual practices are often very much like those found in Judaism, their civic structures resemble those of ancient Egypt, and their beliefs about creation are a close match for an ancient Buddhist tradition.

What we know about the Dogon religion comes out of studies conducted over a span of three decades, beginning in the 1930s, by French anthropologists Marcel Griaule and Germaine Dieterlen. In part because of these studies, Griaule became one of the most well-known and respected anthropologists of his day. Griaule and Dieterlen documented and filmed many aspects of Dogon life and, over a long period of time, succeeded in gaining the trust of the Dogon people. Griaule described the Dogon religion as a closely held secret tradition, one whose mysteries were revealed only to sincere initiates after long years of study with a Dogon priest. Griaule himself was initiated into this secret tradition, became an honorary Dogon citizen, and was given a Dogon burial after his untimely death in 1956.

The Dogon first attracted public attention because of a 1975 book by Robert K. G. Temple called *The Sirius Mystery.* In this book, which was based on a partial translation of Griaule and Dieterlen's study, Temple reported that the Dogon priests were aware of certain obscure astronomical facts about the star system of Sirius that they should not reasonably have known without access to powerful modern telescopes. Sirius is the brightest star in the night sky and was a center of focus in the myths of many ancient cultures. The Dogon knew that Sirius is not one star but two—that the bright star of Sirius (referred to by astronomers as Sirius A) has a dark, small, dense companion dwarf star (Sirius B). They also knew the correct orbital period of fifty years for the two stars. Temple presented this knowledge as evidence of a possible alien contact in ancient times.

As might be expected, Temple's book generated a great deal of controversy, both with the general public and in the scientific world. Carl Sagan (the Cornell University astronomer who became a well-known popularizer of science) discounted the alien aspect of Temple's book and proposed instead that the Dogon priests must have gained their knowledge about Sirius from some modern-day visitor from the outside world. Dieterlen countered Sagan's argument by presenting a four-hundred-year-old carved Dogon artifact that depicted the relationship between the two stars. In the 1980s, a much shorter-term restudy of Griaule's work was conducted by Belgian anthropologist Walter Van Beek. After extensive interviews with a wide range of Dogon informants, Van Beek's team was unable to re-create Griaule's findings. Based on that, he concluded that the tradition must have been fabricated by the Dogon priests on Griaule's behalf. Since my comparative studies rest on Griaule and Dieterlen's anthropological work, one of my critical efforts has been to try to gain a perspective on these challenges to the legitimacy of Griaule's Dogon cosmology.

From our viewpoint, there are several convincing arguments to be made against Sagan's outlook. First, we can see that the Dogon references about the Sirius stars are given in what are arguably ancient Egyptian words, a language that went out of use around 700 BCE. For example, in my view, the Dogon Sigi (or Sigui) festival of Sirius is defined by the Egyptian word *skhai,* which means "to celebrate a festival." So the first problem with Sagan's solution to the question of Dogon knowledge about Sirius would be to suggest a credible modern visitor who would have framed modern astronomical information using such archaic words. Next, in Egyptian mythology the goddess Isis was understood to represent the bright star Sirius, or Sothis. The Egyptians themselves claimed that Isis had a dark sister named Nephthys, and so implied their own knowledge of a second, less luminous Sirius star in ancient times.

The difficulty with Van Beek's conclusion lies with an aligned ritual Dogon shrine called a granary. Griaule and Dieterlen defined this shrine as a kind of grand mnemonic for the Dogon cosmological system, whereas Van Beek considered that concept to be an imagined construct of Griaule's making. The problem is that both the shrine and its associated cosmology are near-perfect matches for a well-known type of Buddhist shrine from India and Asia called a stupa and its cosmology. Since the legitimacy of the Buddhist shrine and its cosmology is well established and has long been well accepted, it simply cannot be possible that the matching Dogon shrine and its related cosmology could have been casual fabrications.

For the purposes of our studies, there are several advantages to using the Dogon system of cosmology as a starting point for our comparisons to other traditions. First, the Dogon are a living culture whose priests have a clear understanding of their own traditions and practices. Also, these Dogon traditions seem to reflect very early practices found in ancient Egypt. For example, the Egyptian hieroglyphic language is thought to have been an early development in dynastic Egypt, whereas the Dogon have never had a native system of writing. The implication is that any relationship between the Dogon and the Egyptians may have ended before writing was introduced. The Dogon also make use of the same set of calendars as were found in ancient Egypt, but without the Egyptian system of five intercalary days to synchronize them. These intercalary days appeared early in Egyptian culture, so this also seems to affirm an earlier relationship for the Dogon with the ancient Egyptians. As we would expect based on that scenario, Dogon culture also shows numerous resemblances to the predynastic Amazigh tribes that resided in Egypt just prior to the First Dynasty (dates for the First Dynasty are ca. 3100–ca. 2890 BCE).

The primary references I rely on for information about Dogon cosmology and language are Griaule's diary of his initiation by a priest into the Dogon tribe, called *Conversations with Ogotemmeli,* and Griaule and Dieterlen's finished study of the Dogon religion, called *The Pale Fox.* My Dogon language references are taken from a French dictionary called *Dictionnaire Dogon.* It was compiled by Griaule's daughter Genevieve Calame-Griaule, who later came to be a respected anthropologist in her own right. I also draw information about Dogon words and practices from numerous articles written over the years by Griaule, Dieterlen, and Calame-Griaule.

My Egyptian language comparisons are based on Sir E. A. Wallis Budge's *An Egyptian Hieroglyphic Dictionary.* This two-volume work was published in 1920 and has since fallen largely out of favor among traditional Egyptologists. However, in my opinion it has the advantage of leaning more toward the African roots of Egyptian words than later dictionaries that rely more on later Greek sources, and so is much more applicable to our purposes. By comparison, if we were studying Shakespeare, we would likely be better served to use a Shakespearean dictionary to interpret archaic word meanings than a modern collegiate dictionary. In any case, Dogon cosmology presents us with the unique opportunity to compare a coherent set of well-defined words with those in Budge's dictionary, and what I have consistently observed is a very close match.

My primary reference for the Buddhist stupa tradition is a work called *The Symbolism of the Stupa* by Adrian Snodgrass. Snodgrass is a professor at the University of Western Sydney, in Australia, and is widely seen as a leading authority on Buddhist architecture and symbolism. I also rely on a second work by Snodgrass called *Architecture, Time, and Eternity,* in which he actually devotes a chapter to the structural and symbolic aspects of the Dogon granary shrine.

There are certain key features of the Dogon cosmological system that enable us to make positive correlations to the Buddhist system and to related cosmological words and concepts in ancient Egypt. The first has to do with how words are defined within the system. Each important term of the cosmology is assigned two or more definitions, and these meanings are logically distanced from one another in such a way so that knowing one meaning will not reasonably allow a person to guess the secondary meanings. As an example, Amma is the name of the Dogon "hidden god," but the word *amma* also means "to grasp, hold firm, or establish." The comparable Egyptian god is called Amen, and the names Amma and Amen are explicitly equated to one another in the languages of various North African tribes. Amen is the name of the Egyptian "hidden god" and can also mean "to establish"[1] Whenever we find these same logically distanced meanings associated with a similar pronunciation in the Egyptian hieroglyphic language, we see justification in arguing that there is a unique correlation. In many cases these meanings may be supported by other evidence, such as a common relationship to the same drawn shape or to comparable deities who have matching icons or who are credited with the same mythic acts. Through these comparisons, we can affirm the meanings of most of the terms of Griaule's Dogon cosmology based on Budge's dictionary. More important, these multiple meanings appear to be linked to cosmological concepts, not to the specific pronunciation of a particular word in any given language. Knowing this allows us to positively correlate Dogon concepts to matching Buddhist concepts, which are given in the markedly different language of Sanskrit.

So from the outset, we know that the Dogon cosmology must be ancient because it matches a Buddhist system that was documented by around 400 BCE and it is given in Egyptian words that were no longer in use after around 700 BCE. We know that neither the Dogon nor the Buddhist system can have changed significantly over time, because if either had, they would no longer match one another. We also know that the meanings Griaule assigns to various Dogon symbols must be substantially correct because of ongoing matches to Buddhist and Egyptian symbols, and we know that his word meanings must be correct because of the match to ancient Egyptian words. So by triangulating on the three systems, we are able to demonstrate the fundamental similarity of the three traditions and to anchor various interpretations we may make in relation to those systems.

Before we begin to correlate references from ancient China to this same cosmology, it is important that we understand the main features of that shared system. One perspective that is common to the traditions we will study is the belief that civilizing skills were imparted to humanity in ancient times by knowledgeable ancestor-teachers or ancestor-gods. Even in ancient Egypt there was a tradition in which the Egyptian hieroglyphic language was understood to have been a gift to Egypt from their mythical gods. In Buddhism, it was understood that Buddha had imparted knowledge to mankind in archaic times. The Dogon also associate eight mythical ancestors with specific civilizing skills and provide specific details about how they were taught. The Na-khi of Tibet credit their Mu ancestors with having brought skills of civilization to mankind. Similar beliefs are commonly expressed by ancient cultures from widespread regions of the globe.

Based on the comparative evidence we have examined, this shared system does seem to have been framed as a civilizing plan, a kind of Peace Corps effort to raise humanity upward from a state of hunter-gatherers to the state of farmers. At the same time, the plan also seems to have been meant to provide us with a creation tradition, one that would help us to understand our place in relation to the larger processes of creation. As such, it centers on three main themes of creation: how the universe was formed, how matter is formed, and how biological reproduction occurs. Comparisons I present in *The Science of the Dogon* suggest that the information relating to these themes of creation was given from a perspective of knowledge and appears to have been entirely scientific.

Because the processes of creation that relate to these three themes are understood to be fundamentally similar to one another, all three were defined in relation to a single set of symbols. So an egg, which represents the starting point for biological reproduction, also came to symbolize the unformed universe prior to the big bang. A clay pot, which can represent a particle of matter in relation to the formation-of-matter theme, also symbolizes a womb in the biological-reproductive theme. Because of the parallel nature of these themes, any interpretation we offer for the meaning of a symbol requires us to first declare which creation theme we are discussing.

It is clear that mnemonics were an important aspect of this ancient creation system. The idea with mnemonics is to associate the concepts we wish to learn with various kinds of memory aids that make it easier to remember them. As an example of how mnemonics work, there was an episode of the 1980s-era television comedy called *Cheers* in which a character named Coach helps a bartender named Sam study for a geography exam. He teaches Sam to set geographical facts about the country of Albania to the tune of the familiar song "When the Saints Go Marching In." The power of mnemonics is such that, having heard the song once during the episode, the audience also learned the facts. The lyrics went:

> *Albania, Albania, you border on the Adriatic,*
> *Your terrain is mostly mountainous,*
> *And your chief export is chrome.*
> *You're a Communist republic.*
> *You're a Red regime.*

In our ancient civilizing plan, concepts of cosmology seem to have been reinforced mnemonically by relating them to structures of daily life. For example, the Dogon and Egyptian civic practice of establishing districts in pairs called "Upper" and "Lower" can be seen to reinforce the cosmological principle of "as above, so below." Concepts of creation are reflected in Dogon agricultural practices, such as their archaic method of plowing a field in the shape of a spiral. Methods of weaving cloth were equated in Dogon culture with ways in which matter is said to be woven. Symbolism was also assigned to various animals and objects of daily life, so that each casual encounter with these objects tended to serve as a reminder for cosmological teachings. Likewise, mythic storylines were tagged to the constellations of stars that would have been in view on any clear night. Concepts of creation that were initially tagged symbolically to objects, animals, and drawn shapes seem to have later been personified into deities. In the Dogon culture, which I believe to be reflective of a very early form of the tradition, only one mythological character rises to the level of an actual deity as we think of them in the classic sense of the word, and that is the Dogon creator-god Amma. Even so, Amma is not personified by the Dogon nor typically portrayed in iconic images.

Within this creation tradition, each symbol represents a stage or concept of creation. When discussing a symbol as it relates to one of the three creative themes, we also need to place that symbol in its proper relationship to other symbolic stages of creation. To help us do that, the Dogon define a series of four-stage metaphors that serve to categorize the symbols. As an example, the Dogon priests discuss four stages of a construction project that compare to four stages of the creative process. In the first stage, called *bummo*, the project is initially framed simply as a conceptual plan. In the second stage, *yala*, the corner points of the structure to be built are marked on the ground with stones that mark its major features. At the third stage, called *tonu*, the ground plan of the structure is refined with more stones to give its outline more precise definition. At the fourth and final stage, called *toy* or *toymu*, the structure is actually built and brought to completion.

A number of four-stage metaphors that follow this same pattern are given to define other classes of symbols. One of these is expressed in terms of the formation of matter, which from a scientific standpoint begins as waves, but then is transformed by an act of perception into what we see as vibrating particles. This metaphor is expressed in terms of the familiar progression of water, fire, wind, and earth, terms that we see as symbolic of waves, an act of perception, vibration, and mass or matter. The metaphor suggests that ancient symbols that relate to water pertain to the early stages of matter, while those that are given in terms of earth relate to the final stages of matter.

Similar four-stage metaphors are given based on other frames of reference. One involves an egg, a gosling chick, a standing goose, and a flying goose. Another is expressed in terms of a seed, the young shoot of a plant, the stem of a growing plant, and a grown plant. Yet another is given in relation to categories of creatures of the animal kingdom, beginning with insects, then fish, then domesticated animals, and finally birds. The four stages of this particular metaphor help us to interpret the symbolism of animal-headed Egyptian deities, where the beetle-headed Kheper represents an initial stage of creation when non-existence transforms into existence, and the bird-headed Thoth represents a finalized stage symbolized by the concept of the Word.

From the Dogon perspective, matter exists in three conceptual worlds. In the First World, matter exists in the perfectly ordered state of primordial waves. In the Second World, comparable to the Egyptian underworld, the waves are disrupted and then fundamentally reorganized. These reorganizational processes produce what the Dogon call the "egg of the world," a structure that exists at every point in space-time, comparable to the Calabi-Yau space in the string theory of modern physics. In the Third World, which coincides with our everyday reality, matter is considered to be a mere reflected image of the underlying waves. Here matter culminates in the form of the *po*, an atom-like structure from which all things are made.

There are certain principles that Griaule says also underlie this system of creation and that again seem to be scientific. These include a principle of duality and the pairing of opposites. These principles are expressed symbolically in a number of different ways, such as opposing colors, like black and white, or opposite sexes, male and female. We see these same principles reflected in certain classic oppositions, such as the notion of the separation of earth and sky.

The very similarly aligned Dogon granary and Buddhist stupa are ritual structures that stand as grand symbols of the cosmology. Because the two structures are effectively counterparts to one another, we will often discuss the two as if they are of a single type. A number of different symbolic concepts of the cosmology and organizational concepts for society are tagged to the structure. The base plan of the structure is defined by geometry that is understood to re-create the initial processes of creation, described as the method by which multiplicity arises from unity. The method of alignment for the structure evokes a series of matching shapes that carry the same cosmological symbolism in both cultures. Each structure also defines two axes that are aligned to the cardinal points of north, south, east, and west and that symbolize the *axis mundi,* or axis of the world. In each case, the base plan is measured out in relation to cubits, a symbolic unit of measure that constitutes one of the signatures of our tradition, meaning that wherever we find cubits, we are likely to find evidence of the influence of our cosmology. Because the symbolism of the structure rests on relationships between various geometric forms, the cubit evolved as a relative unit of measure, one whose length can vary from culture to culture, and sometimes even within a single culture.

2
EARLY CHINESE CONCEPTS OF COSMOLOGY

It makes sense that we begin our exploration of ancient Chinese cosmology with the initiating stage of creation as it is defined in the Dogon cosmological plan—the idea of creation from water. As in Egypt, Africa, India, and Tibet, Chinese concepts of creation begin with the notion of an undifferentiated watery chaos, from which all material things ultimately emerge. This watery mass is said to exist either outside of or prior to the beginning of time and is thought to be the ongoing source of all creation.[1] This Chinese concept of chaos, expressed by the word *luan,* although often also applied to issues of chaos in the real world, is in many ways a match for the Egyptian concept of the primordial waters as characterized by the concept of *nun.* A similar concept exists in Dogon cosmology, where the root *nu* refers to the cosmological concept of water or waves. This same pronunciation also arguably provides the phonetic value for Egyptian glyphs that depict the image of a wave 𓈖 or waves 𓈗.

A description of the Chinese concept of luan, which is similar in many ways to the concept of primal chaos as we understand it in other ancient cosmologies we have studied, is given by Brian J. Bruya of Eastern Michigan University:

[In the] Chinese notion of chaotic disorder (*luan*), early Daoists posit a type of chaos that is to be cultivated rather than feared. This chaos is a primal disorder, akin to Hesiod's, but rather than threatening disruption, it is replete with creative potential and through spontaneous action yields orderly processes that proceed from the concretion of things to their dissolution and back, in a complex web of relations. This processional activity, although taken in one sense as cosmogonic, in a more important sense is immanent at every moment of activity.[2]

Likewise, in China creation is understood to have arisen from this chaos through a process of geometric division—the same process by which multiplicity is thought to have emerged from unity in other cosmologies. This process of differentiation is deemed necessary to produce an ordered space.[3] It is this same process that is said to be replicated symbolically by the plan of aligned ritual structures such as the Buddhist stupa and Dogon granary, which are central symbols in the Buddhist and Dogon cosmologies. According to Adrian Snodgrass, one of the stated purposes of the stupa plan is to illustrate how unity evokes multiplicity. Snodgrass tells us that, in the stupa tradition, the concept of multiplicity is associated symbolically with the geometry that produces a circle.[4] We find this same notion expressed symbolically in the Egyptian word *at,* which Budge defines as meaning "multitudinous," a word that we take as a synonym for the concept of multiplicity. Using our method of interpreting Egyptian words, in which associated concepts are substituted for glyphs, the word reads "that which ⎛ gives or makes ⌢ a circle ◯."[5]

This evolution from one to many is reflected in the plan of the matching Dogon granary structure as a progression in which a single initiating impulse causes a creator-god (who is himself considered to be dual in nature) to evoke four primordial elements that are, in turn, associated with eight ancestor-gods. The mathematical progression of 1-2-4-8 replicates a process of creation called mitosis, whereby a fertilized egg divides again and again as a function of biological reproduction. On another level—still in keeping with the Chinese symbolism—it is also Snodgrass's contention that the act of building a stupa is understood to represent the act of distinguishing an ordered space from a disordered field.

A similar view of the nature of this undifferentiated primordial chaos in earliest Chinese cosmology is provided by Mark Edward Lewis in *The Construction of Space in Early China,* given in essentially the same terms. Lewis writes:

> The early Chinese themselves had already developed discourses dealing with the historical construction of ordered human space. These began from the image of a primal state of undifferentiated chaos out of which all objects and ultimately human society emerged. Perhaps the most influential was a cosmogonic discourse preserved as a complete narrative in four texts, as well as in scattered references. These describe a formless, watery chaos at the beginning of time, and then depict the emergence of objects through a process of sequential division. This is sometimes described in mathematical terms as the division of an original unity into two parts, then three or four, ending in the formation of all things. While these divisions are not the work of men, the texts repeatedly insist that only the sage could understand the principles underlying this emergence of ordered space.[6]

Working from a similar concept of a primordial wavelike mass that exists outside of space and time (one that is seen as inherently organized, rather than chaotic), Dogon concepts of how matter is formed evoke the three mythical worlds of matter: a perfectly ordered First World of waves (or of a watery chaos), a disrupted and reorderd Second World, and our Third World, which is a reflection of the waves of the First World.

We have several perspectives from which to correlate the Dogon

Second World of matter to the Egyptian underworld. Both are imagined to be below our plane of existence. Both worlds are governed by a jackal, who symbolizes the concept of disorder. The Egyptian underworld, or Tuat (or Duat), is symbolized by the image of a star in a circle ⊕̣, a figure that is essentially a match for the drawing made by the Dogon priests to represent the final stage of this reordered Second World of matter. The Dogon refer to this figure as the egg of the world.

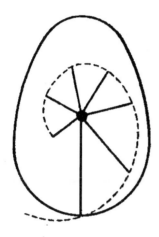

Figure 2.1. The Dogon egg of the world

The Daoist concept of *hundun* (sometimes given as *kunlun*), which can also be seen as an alternate expression of this same primordial chaos, defines a *noumenal* world (a world beyond our observation, whose attributes we can therefore only infer) that is the conceptual opposite of our *phenomenal* world. These worlds are conceived of as opposing aspects of essence and substance, the same two terms that are explicitly assigned to the hemisphere-like Dogon and Buddhist ritual shrines—terms that we correlate to mass and matter. Ancient Chinese cosmological thought projects its notion of creation worlds in a somewhat modified and perhaps more immediately practical way, wherein the multiple spheres of daily life—those of the individual, the family, the community, the region, and the nation—are all interpreted as distinct levels of creation.[7] Some references on Chinese cosmology make a distinction between the concept of luan, which is defined as implying the notion of disorder, and the concept of hundun, which refers to chaos. This makes sense from the Dogon perspective, where the underlying chaos of the First World of matter is considered to be perfectly ordered, while disorder—comparable to the initial mess a person might make in the process of reorganizing a closet—is what characterizes their Second World.

In his work *Myth and Meaning in Early Daoism: The Theme of Chaos (Hundun)*, Norman J. Girardot equates the two concepts of hundun and kunlun and defines them as "a watery, fluid, or embryonic state; a primordial whirlpool or abyss" that was "closed up like an egg." He relates this concept in China to the notion of a calabash gourd, which was one of the first cultivated plants in the world and which also plays a mythic role in the Dogon creation tradition. Girardot tells us that the primordial abyss of kunlun was described as having "two tiers: an upright cone matched with a reversed cone."[8] This is the same description given by the Dogon priests to their conception of what the unformed universe was like prior to their counterpart to the big bang (figure 2.2). Quoting from my own book *The Cosmological Origins of Myth and Symbol:*

> [The Dogon myths] describe the universe as having begun as a tiny ball of unrealized potential called *Amma's egg.* According to the Dogon priests, this ball—which housed all of the *seeds or signs* of the future universe—swirled and intensified while being seeded, yet somehow also held in stasis for a very long time by two "thorns." As the speed of the spinning egg intensified, it became more difficult to maintain equilibrium and so the egg eventually ruptured and released a whirlwind that scattered primordial matter to all corners of the universe.[9]

We gain potential insight into the source of the dual Chinese terms for this chaos, *hundun* and *kunlun,* by turning to Genevieve Calame-Griaule's *Dictionnaire Dogon.* There we find that the Dogon word for "calabash" is *kodu* and that the Dogon word *kunu* refers to "the egg of the world prior to the expansion of its germs." The suggestion is that the Chinese terms may represent a comparable pairing: one term

*Figure 2.2. Dogon
"thorns" of the
unformed universe*

that likely referred to the concept of a calabash gourd, the other to the unformed universe.

In the plan of ancient cosmology as we understand it, concepts of the formation of the universe are treated as a theme that is separate from—although in many ways parallel to—concepts relating to the genesis of matter. While the universe is conceived of as a kind of cosmogonic egg, matter in its primordial wavelike state is conceptualized as a watery mass. Both constructs are deemed to have existed before, beyond, or outside of the confines of space and time, and both represent distinct processes by which space and time are thought to have come into existence, and so lend themselves to separate treatment. It is significant that, in regard to the familiar phrase "as above, so below," it is these two themes—one macroscopic and the other microscopic—that appear to correspond to the cosmological terms *above* and *below,* respectively. As understood in the Dogon and Buddhist cosmologies, the sequential processes by which space initially comes to be ordered are reflected in the geometry that is traditionally used to align a Buddhist stupa and a Dogon granary. This geometry plays out in the method by which an initiate is taught to orient the shrine, which for both the Dogon and the Buddhists serves as a kind of grand mnemonic for their cosmologies (figure 2.3).

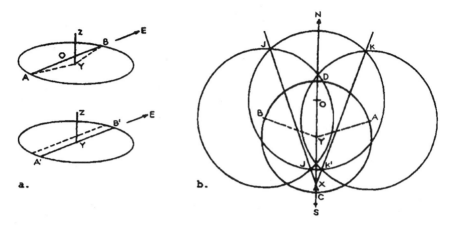

Figure 2.3. The determination of the orient (from Snodgrass,
The Symbolism of the Stupa, *15)*

The figure begins with a stick, or gnomon, that defines the center of a drawn circle and forms what is essentially a sundial, a tool that can be used to track the motion of the sun and the hours of the day. The stick's two longest shadows of the day (which occur in the morning and the evening) are marked at their point of intersection with the circle. A line drawn between these points is inherently aligned to define an east-west axis. Two more slightly larger circles—centered on these same two points—intersect each other to create the endpoints of a second line perpendicular to the first, which therefore defines a north-south axis.

The cubit was the unit of measure used to define the symbolic structures of both the Buddhist stupa and the Dogon granary, and so it can be said to be intimately associated with our theoretic plan of cosmology. Like most cosmological terms defined within this plan, the concept of a cubit is presented with two distinct definitions: it is described both as the distance from the elbow to the tip of the middle finger and as the average pace or step of a person. As such, the cubit would represent a distance that could be readily marked out by most initiates without the need for tools. In Dogon cosmology, the cubit also takes on the role of a measure of the heavens when a mythic character named Ogo is said to "measure out the universe" in eight billion "steps." Based on the second definition given above, the term *step* can be taken as a symbolic reference within the myth to the cubit. As we might expect, the concept of a cubit was understood in essentially the same terms in ancient China, where it was described as a "heaven measuring unit."[10]

It is important to understand that the cubit as defined within our cosmology represents a relative unit of measure, not a measure of standardized precision. Since the symbolic meanings of these aligned ritual structures depend primarily on relationships between the geometric figures they evoke, the alignments they facilitate, and the cosmological meanings that are overtly assigned to them, any measured differences in the actual lengths of cubits as they were applied by various cultures or initiates are unimportant. None of the cosmological symbolism depends on the precise length at which a cubit may have been measured. Algernon Edward Berriman, the author of the seminal work *Historical Metrology*, defines widely varying lengths for the cubits of different cultures. He also tells us that the Egyptian royal cubit is defined by the semidiagonal of a square (the distance from the center of the square to any corner) that measures ten Roman feet in perimeter, and by the radius of a circle ten Assyrian feet in circumference. In other words, for Berriman the concept of a cubit is, like the base plan of the stupa structure itself, intimately associated with the concept of the squaring of a circle.[11]

The notion of squaring a circle plays a role in the early geometry of civilizations, such as ancient Egypt, and in the cosmologies of many ancient cultures. The figures of the circle and the square are treated as symbols in relation to various stages of creation, and so the idea of reconciling one shape with the other implies the notion of reconciling or equating two concepts.

An important theme of the Dogon and Buddhist cosmologies that is also reflected in the cosmologies of other cultures emphasizes the significance of the four cardinal directions, knowledge of which was a prerequisite to the proper ordering of space. Although alignments to individual stars were common, it was often according to the four compass directions of north, south, east, and west that the ritual shrines and temples of ancient cultures were oriented. An important step in the method of alignment of a Buddhist stupa, as I have described it, involves the determination of an axis. The concept of the four directional meridians is often expressed in the cosmologies of ancient cultures using the phrase "axis of the world," or axis mundi. In China, the earliest cosmological models for which we have evidence were based on ritual structures that were also aligned to the four cardinal directions, also defined in terms of an axis.[12]

The ancient concept of four directions was sometimes expressed with the phrase "pillars of the world." These pillars were structures that were imagined to exist in relation to the four compass points and were imagined to support space or to separate earth from sky. There are Chinese myths in which the mother goddess Nu-wa (whose name is sometimes given as Nu-gua) is credited with having repaired or restored the "fallen" pillars of the world. Inscriptions from the Shang dynasty (which date from perhaps as early as 1700 BCE) indicate a strong concern with the center and four directions—concepts that are also of great importance in the Dogon and Buddhist cosmologies.

Paul Wheatley of the University of Chicago tells us in his classic text *The Pivot of the Four Quarters* that several key concepts, central to the cosmologies we have studied, were also apparent in ancient China. These concepts include the notion that the reality we perceive simply mimics or reflects the attributes of a more fundamental, underlying reality and the concept that profane or disordered space must be made sacred by systematically reordering and realigning it in relation to a world axis, or axis mundi. This reordering of space begins with a defined center and is conceived of as extending outward to the four cardinal points. These concepts are also associated, within the confines of what Wheatley refers to as an "astrobiological conceptual framework," with rituals that define a kind of harmony between those processes that occur within the *microcosm* and those that happen in the *macrocosm*.[13] Again, this is the concept that I feel is implicit in the phrase that practically defines our plan of cosmology: as above, so below.

Just as the center point of the stupa plan can be used to track the hours of the day, so the east-west line it defines can be used to track the seasons of the year, and so the same figure that serves as a sundial can also function as an effective calendar. On two days of the year—the two equinoxes—this east-west line will pass through the central stick, or gnomon. Thereafter, the line will move progressively farther away from the stick until we reach the date of the next solstice, at which point the line's direction of movement will reverse itself. Daily observance of the position of this line would allow an initiate to pinpoint and effectively track the starting dates and duration of each of the seasons and to establish a correct length for the year. Such tools of time measurement would have been a necessary prerequisite to the establishment of any well-regulated agriculture.

Both the Dogon and the Buddhists associate the circular base of their aligned structure and its defined center with the sun. Both explicitly say that the circular base represents the sun. Knowledge of this overt symbolism and the timekeeping functions it facilitates makes it easy to see why various ancient cultures might have chosen to adopt a written sun glyph of similar shape. In Egypt, this shape ⊙ is associated with the sun god Ra. In the earliest carved-bone system of writing in China, called oracle bone script, the shape takes the form of a glyph, pronounced "ri" (figure 2.4). The Hollow Earth website notes, "The ancient oracle bone script depiction of the word for 'sun,' or 'ri,' is a circle with a dot in it. This gradually morphed into the symbol used today in traditional Chinese writing."[14]

Figure 2.4. Left: Ri, the glyph for "sun" in oracle bone script, was written as a circle with a dot in it. Right: The modern Chinese symbol for the sun is similar.

The same circular figure that serves as the base plan of a stupa and of the Dogon granary can be seen as an alternate expression of the egg-in-a-ball figure that is the conceptual starting point for creation within Dogon cosmology. The Dogon priests alternately refer to this figure as the womb of all world signs and as the picture of Amma, the Dogon creator-god (figure 2.5).

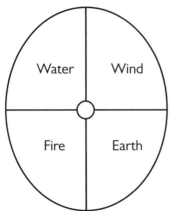

Figure 2.5. The Dogon figure representing the womb of all world signs, which is also a representation of Amma

As explained by the Dogon priests, Amma resides in the center of the figure and evokes the four primordial elements of water, fire, wind, and earth. The circle is divided by two intersecting lines into four quadrants, each associated with one of these elements, and, cosmologically, the lines are considered to be a two-dimensional representation of the axis mundi. When viewed from the alternate perspective of biological creation, the point of intersection of these two lines is seen to symbolize the umbilicus, or *omphalos munde,* the "navel of the world."

In Dogon cosmology, the four primordial elements are defined as water, fire, wind, and earth. One can interpret these elements to represent four states of matter (liquid, plasma, gas, and solid mass), but as the Dogon priests define the processes of creation, it becomes clear that they are also meant to symbolize four distinct stages in the formation of matter. From a scientific perspective, water represents matter in its wavelike form, fire represents an act of perception (the act that initiates a transformation of matter into particle form), wind represents the concept of vibration, and earth represents the concept of mass.

Figure 2.6 offers a visual representation of the central concepts of Daoist cosmology. Many of the concepts and geometric shapes that are central to the alignment of a Buddhist stupa, as well as key elements

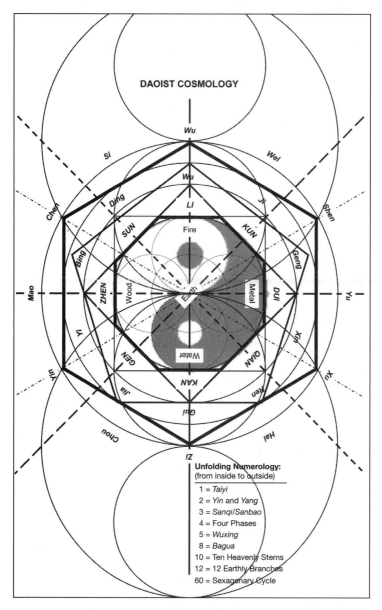

Figure 2.6. Elements of Daoist cosmology depicted as geometrical relationships (from Daozhan: Divination Resource for Daoist Calculation, *by Michael Hamilton)*

found in the Dogon egg-in-a-ball figure, are evident in the diagram. These include the notion of alignment to the cardinal points based on an axis, the derivation of which is accomplished in relation to a series of geometric figures. The Daoist diagram also illustrates the concept of squaring a circle, which is a geometric principle that underlies the plan of the Dogon and Buddhist shrines. Furthermore, the diagram reflects symbolism that is given in terms of the primordial elements, which are again foundational to the Dogon and Buddhist cosmologies. Our view is that this group of symbolic elements, evoked in terms of this specific geometry, constitutes one of the unmistakable signatures of our cosmological plan.

Although the concepts of Daoism are often expressed in terms of five primordial elements (only four are typically enumerated in the Dogon and Egyptian systems), these five elements (earth, water, fire, metal, and wood) are given in reference to a five-pointed star figure that is reminiscent of the figure familiarly used to symbolize the Egyptian underworld ⊕ (figure 2.7). These five elements are also given in a sequential relationship that seems sensible to us within the context of other cosmologies we have studied. Wood is defined symbolically as "what fire burns." Metal can be seen as the next conceptual stage of matter beyond the emergence of mass.

There is a third aspect to Dogon cosmological thought that relates to the creation of the universe as distinct from the processes that form matter. The Dogon priests postulate the existence in primordial times

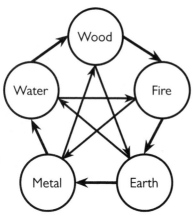

Figure 2.7. Chinese primordial elements conceived as five points of a star

of a primordial egg, which was said to have held all of the "seeds or signs" of the future universe. They say that an undefined force caused this egg to open, scattering matter—like pellets of clay—to all corners of the universe. From a scientific viewpoint, this is essentially the story of the big bang, which also attributes the origins of the universe to a kind of primordial rupture.

In China, one tradition holds that the universe formed in chaos, then coalesced into a kind of cosmogonic egg. Held in balance within the egg were the opposing principles of yin and yang, along with a mythical giant named Pan-gu. One variation on the Chinese myth portrays a doglike Pan-gu as a sleeping giant who woke and stretched and broke the egg; another says that he succeeded in opening the egg by swinging his axe. (The symbol of the adze or axe also plays a symbolic role in facilitating the processes of creation in the Dogon and Egyptian cosmological systems.) In these myths, Pan-gu, who, like the Dogon creator-god Amma, is described as having a dual nature and as embodying both male and female attributes, is considered to be the first living being and the creator of all things. The concept of yin and yang is reminiscent of the principle of paired opposites that is upheld in the Dogon and Buddhist cosmologies and that is also central to modern scientific concepts of the formation of matter.[15]

Symbolism, which we characterize as the original language of ancient cosmology, presents itself in China in many of the same essential ways in which we find it in each of the other cosmologies we have compared. Throughout this volume I will cite examples of Chinese symbols and symbolic concepts that lend themselves to side-by-side comparison with matching symbols from other cosmological traditions. These include glyphs with matched meanings, matching numerological symbolism, comparable symbolism assigned through myth, parallel symbolic concepts, examples of mythological characters who perform similar acts, and so on. Sinologists also recognize the cosmological symbolism that plays out in the architecture of aligned ritual structures.[16] In some cases, the resemblances to symbolic elements of the cosmologies we will have previously discussed will seem so very obvious as to not always require special mention.

Another important feature of the cosmologies we have compared lies in the ways in which meanings are assigned to words. Egyptologists often take notice (from their perspective) of the tendency of the ancient Egyptian priests to make use of puns. This apparent feature of Egyptian writings is a consequence of the many Egyptian words that appear to be homonyms of one another—words that are pronounced alike but spelled differently. However, from the perspective of Dogon culture, where written language never actually developed (and so questions of spelling become moot), the Egyptian homonyms are understood as the alternate meanings that are assigned to important cosmological terms. A similar situation exists with earliest written Chinese language, where word pairings and complementary meanings also play out in the eyes of researchers like wordplay and puns.[17]

A seminal myth of ancient Egypt describes how Osiris (a deity whom we associate with the civilizing skills of our cosmological plan) was tricked, trapped, killed, and dismembered. His body parts were said to have been widely scattered across all parts of ancient Egypt. In one version of the myth, his son Horus (whom we associate with the concept of a symbol based on Egyptian language references) was able to gather up these widespread pieces in an attempt to reconstitute Osiris. This, in practice, is the actual role of the comparative cosmologist, who, using symbols, attempts to redefine the contours of an ancient cosmology by piecing together its diverse elements.

3
ANCESTOR-TEACHERS IN THE CHINESE COSMOLOGY

One important concept associated with the cosmologies we have studied is the belief in a set of revered ancestor-teachers (or ancestor-gods) who are credited with bringing instructed civilizing skills to humanity in ancient times. Overt references to this belief can be found in each of the cultures we have studied. Often—and sometimes to the confusion of some researchers—there seem to be both historical and symbolic aspects to these ancestors, evidence for which often predates the advent of written history in any given culture. Consequently these ancestors may be somewhat vaguely interpreted as having been quasi-historical or quasi-mythical in nature. On one level, they may be treated as actual historical figures, as now-mythical kings or patriarchs who lived and are credited with important acts. In some cultures, they may even be treated as deified beings. However, it has become apparent from our studies of ancient cosmology that the word *ancestor* can also be a carefully applied symbolic term that is used to define important concepts of creation.

The Dogon trace their culture to a set of mythical ancestor-teachers who are said to have been the patriarchs of eight honored family lineages. According to the Dogon priests, these human Dogon ancestors acquired their knowledge from nonhuman teachers who were spiritual, rather than physical, in nature and who, out of concern for the perceived dangers their own prolonged presence might inflict on their human students, decided to present their teachings indirectly. They opted to sequester eight Dogon ancestors, taking them away from the rest of the tribe and instructing them in important civilizing skills, then returning them, now competent to instruct the remainder of the tribe.

Like all good cosmological words of the Dogon creation tradition, the term *ancestor* carries several different meanings depending on the context in which it is given. The first meaning is given in its literal and familiar sense, where it seems to define a set of honored historical figures who were founders of the Dogon tribe. In this context, the Dogon Lebe, which is the name of one of the Dogon ancestors and is assigned to one of their revered families, might be seen as a functional counterpart to the Hebrew tribe Levi. Likewise, the Dogon priests, referred to by the title *hogon,* might be seen as counterparts to the priestly *cohanes* of Judaism. From this perspective, the term *ancestor* refers to an older family relative who lived *before you*. (Considered in this way, the past is conceptualized by the Dogon as being *in front of us*, while the future is pictured as being behind. This concept, although perhaps counterintuitive to our own cultural view, makes sense if you visualize your ancestors as a long line of passengers filing off a bus, with the oldest relative stepping off first.)

From the standpoint of the biological theme of Dogon cosmology, the term *ancestor* refers to a kind of filial heritage that would be akin to genetics in science. In this view, the symbolic term *ancestor* can be understood as referring to a concept akin to a gene in the science of reproductive biology. It is understood by the Dogon priests that people can see traits that resemble their ancestors in themselves and in their children because of this biologically based ancestral heritage. Taken together, these perspectives of Dogon cosmology leave us with a view of ancestors who might represent mythical teachers, who might have been historical heads of families or tribes, or who may represent scientifically sensible concepts presented within the context of a symbolic cosmology. In other words, the Dogon ancestors—like those of ancient China—could be aptly described as being, all at once, quasi-historical, quasi-scientific, and quasi-mythical in nature.

Evidence of the concept of ancestors in China goes back to the earliest oracle bone writings of the Shang dynasty (which begin around 1700 BCE) and has come down to us as two lists or lineages of names. The first list belongs to what are called high ancestors, who seem to have been endowed with magic powers, and the second to immediate ancestors, who are treated in more historical terms as people who may have actually lived. The names in these ancestor lists are given without accompanying backstories, and so we often have no ascribed actions or attributes to associate with them. The suggestion is that the writings honor a group of mythical personages from the remote past who were, at some later time, joined to or intermingled with a historical genealogy. Both groups are equally considered to be "ancestors," and there are no overt references by which to firmly designate the high ancestors as having been gods as opposed to ordinary men.[1] Within this context, the Chinese perspective on the concept of ancestors seems to be largely consistent with the concept as it is presented in the Dogon culture.

In China, we are also told that the names of the earliest ancestral kings of the Shang dynasty (1766 BCE–1122 BCE) were based on ten oracle bone glyph characters that were used to signify the ten days of the week. We may recall from our discussion in prior volumes that the ancient Egyptians also observed a ten-day week. In China, these inscribed characters were referred to by the term *shi ri,* which means "ten suns." The term consists of two written symbols—the Chinese glyph for the number ten and the sun glyph, which originally presented the same appearance as the Egyptian sun glyph, but in its modern incarnation takes on the form of a squared version of the Egyptian glyph (see figure 2.4 on p. 29). Like the Egyptian sun glyph, the Chinese character is traditionally interpreted to mean "sun" and "day" and to designate concepts of time. The two glyphs of the Chinese word for "week" mirror the spelling of the Egyptian word *met,* which also means "week."

We have surmised that the Egyptian word can be read symbolically as "ten days" and that the glyphs thereby constitute a symbolic definition of an Egyptian week. However, given the multiple meanings that are assigned to the Egyptian sun glyph, the word could as easily be interpreted alternately to mean "ten suns," as does its counterpart in ancient China. In both cases, the symbols that comprise the words seem to define the meaning of the word *week* symbolically and are given in the same contextual relationship to documented observances of a ten-day week. It is also traditionally accepted that, as in ancient Egypt, a 360-day year was observed during the Shang dynasty in China.[2] So from the standpoint of calendars and written glyph symbolism, the Chinese references that serve to associate the concept of ancestors to the days of the week and the concept of a week to written language seem to run largely parallel to those in ancient Egypt.

In the Dogon culture, the cosmological import of the term *ancestor* is conveyed in yet another way, again through the same drawing that we have referred to as the egg in a ball, the womb of all world signs, or the picture of Amma (see figure 2.5 in chapter 2). From this perspective, the Dogon priests associate the concept of ancestors with the progressive divisions of the egg in a ball. The Dogon creator-god Amma, who is considered to be dual in nature, occupies the center of the figure; Amma represents the conceptual egg that is surrounded and enclosed by the outer ball. Each of the four primordial elements evoked by Amma (water, fire, wind, and earth) is associated with a pair of ancestors who are themselves interpreted to represent opposing aspects of their respective element. The pair of ancestors associated with water represents water in its liquid form and as water vapor. Those associated with fire represent light versus darkness (or for some cultures fire and wood, an assignment that we said is given from the perspective that wood is "what fire burns"). The ancestors associated with wind represent still air and air in motion. Those associated with earth represent mass versus space, or—in the language of myth—earth and sky. Remnants of comparable symbolism that is also seemingly couched in the opposing aspects of the primordial elements can be seen to play out in regard to the paired Ennead and Ogdoad deities in ancient Egypt.

These male and female ancestors reflect the previously mentioned Dogon cosmological principle of the pairing of opposites. Taken from the perspective of the biological theme of creation, the pairings are supportive of the genetic symbolism we already associate with these ancestors, where—through the reproductive processes of meiosis—a half set of genes from the father's sperm combines with a half set of genes from the mother's egg to produce the complete DNA set of a new individual.

In Egypt, we are presented with two outwardly inconsistent myths of creation that define eight ancestral deities as emergent pairs. In the first, a creator-god is said to have evoked eight ancestor-gods after having performed a masturbatory act. (In the Dogon tradition, the creator-god Amma initiates the processes of creation with an incestuous or masturbatory act.) In the second Egyptian myth, the creation of these deities is explicitly assigned to the mother goddess Neith, who is overtly credited with having given birth to all of the later Egyptian deities. However, we can see based on the Dogon model of cosmology that, from a biological perspective, the tradition describes processes of creation that center on events that transpire inside a womb. From a mythological standpoint, this womb would likely belong to the mother goddess, or in ancient Egyptian terms, Neith. By this interpretation, Neith can be understood to be intimately involved in both mythic storylines: one that seems to be given from an astrocosmological point of view and the other from a biological viewpoint. But from the apparent perspective of the cellular reproductive processes described in the second version of the myth, Neith plays no credited role because, as the owner of the womb, she is simply too large to fit in the picture. We conclude that it is because of the concurrent symbolism of these dual themes that the Dogon egg in a ball is alternately described as a womb and that the axis mundi symbolism is given alternately as an "umbilicus munde." Recognition of these concurrent symbolic themes allows us to reconcile an outward contradiction in the Egyptian creation myths, in which a creator-god is ostensibly credited with having evoked the first Egyptian deities, yet, alternately, the birth of these same gods and goddesses is overtly credited to the mother goddess Neith.

In similar fashion, Chinese cosmology recognizes a Neith-like mother goddess named Nu-wa. Like Neith in Egypt, Nu-wa is also associated with concepts of biological reproduction. Ancient Chinese records suggest that the time of Nu-wa, like that of Neith in Egypt, preceded all other stages of creation. As we would expect, Nu-wa is associated with the primordial waters that underlie creation. Acts credited to Nu-wa repeat themes and symbolism found in the Dogon creation tradition. For example, Nu-wa is said to have created humans from clay, a familiar mythic theme that is often repeated in the creation traditions of many different cultures.

In the earliest myths of China, the role of ancestral teacher is played by the three Mythical Sovereigns (who are sometimes referred to as the Three Sage Kings or the Three August Ones) and the Five Virtuous Emperors (who are sometimes referred to as the Five Emperors). Depending on the source and because of inherent uncertainties that exist within the surviving evidence in China, there can be wide variations in how these roles are assigned to individual personages. For example, Paul Wheatley tells us that the Sage Kings Yao and Shun are completely absent from the earliest Chinese texts, yet they are given precedence in the traditional chronology. The situation is further confused by the fact that some characters have been identified in different ways in different epochs of Chinese history. Yu the Great was treated as a creator-god in the early Chou period but by the end of that period was deemed to have been a human king.[3]

Consequently, we cannot even provide a definitive list of which personages actually constitute the Three Sage Kings or the Five Virtuous Emperors because the players change so amorphously, depending on the viewpoint of the individual researcher or the period of the textual evidence that is involved. Likewise, depending on the outlook of the researcher, candidates for these positions can sometimes cross categories and consequently may appear on either of the two lists. This means that, for the purposes of our study, the best we can hope to do is review the attributes of the likeliest mythological characters who typically populate these lists and state from the outset that our purpose here is not to try to reconcile these differences in outlook but only to shed whatever new light we can on the subject based on direct comparison to the other cosmologies we have studied.

One point of departure for us in our discussion of these ancestors might be to examine the key terms that survive in Chinese cosmology, since our experience has been that these concepts seem to hold true from culture to culture and across languages. This knowledge provides us with a way to potentially circumvent some of the insufficiencies of evidence that we are presented with in China, simply by correlating the Chinese term to matching terms in the other cosmologies and pursuing any promising associations we might ultimately find.

As an example of this approach, we might explore the Chinese terms *sage* and *virtuous* to see if either of those concepts carry cosmological symbolism. We know that in Egypt the term *sage* is expressed by the word *tchaasu,* which is based on the phonetic root *tchaas,* meaning "primeval wisdom, the wisdom of ancient times."[4] The concept of virtues is expressed by the Egyptian word *aakhu.* The *aakhut* were the "wise instructed folk" of ancient Egypt whom we already associate with the ancestor-teachers of the Dogon.[5] From this perspective, these Chinese designations provide one possible set of links to the Dogon and Egyptian ancestor traditions.

In the prevailing view of the Chinese scholars, the first of the eight Chinese ancestors is the legendary king Fu-xi, or Fu-hsi, who is traditionally paired with the mother goddess Nu-wa. Symbolism supports the traditional pairing of these two mythical beings in that the Chinese term *nu* means "woman" and *fu* means "husband." There are many ancient Chinese stories that offer differing versions of the identity of Fu-xi, and so his precise nature cannot be firmly given. Some consider him to have been a god of creativity, associated with arts and crafts.

Traditionally, he is said to have invented methods of fire making and of fishing and trapping. He is also credited with having invented the eight trigrams of the *Yijing,* or *I Ching,* which are traditionally said to symbolize eight natural phenomena, including the primordial elements of water, fire, wind, and earth. In accordance with our view that cosmological shapes may have been adopted as some of the earliest written characters of the early symbolic languages, it makes sense that Fu-xi was also said to have developed the first of the Chinese written characters, and so—like the gods of ancient Egypt—he can be said to have been responsible for the introduction of written language in China.[6] References to Fu-xi in China are dated to as early as 2850 BCE, or roughly contemporaneous with early dynastic Egypt.[7]

In the course of our previous cosmological studies as they relate to ancient language, we have uncovered a number of apparent conventions that have proved useful when trying to interpret symbolic references in the cosmologies of other cultures. Recognition of two of these conventions came out of discussions that I initiated with North African ethnologist Helene Hagan early in my Dogon studies. In her book *The Shining Ones* she draws parallels between words and symbols of the predynastic Amazigh tribes (ancestors to the modern-day Berbers, who lived in Egypt prior to the First Dynasty) and those found in ancient Egypt. The first of these conventions is based on a realization, which we arrived at cooperatively, that priestly titles in both the Dogon and Amazigh cultures center on a root word that means "light." This is a concept that is also expressed by the word *aakhu* in Egypt, which is also the name of the Egyptian light god. The Egyptian word *aakhu* is a likely correlate to the Dogon word *ogo,* which forms the root of several important Dogon cosmological terms, including the word Dogon itself.

In the mythological storyline of Dogon cosmology, a character named Ogo, whose name means "quick," plays the apparent role of light in the creation myth, while his twin sister seems to play the role of time. Ogo imagines that he can create a universe as perfect as the one made by the Dogon creator-god Amma and proceeds to break off a square piece of the placenta of Amma. (Dogon and Buddhist symbolism suggests that, from one symbolic perspective, the figure of a square can symbolize the concept of space.) One consequence of Ogo's act is that it ends up separating him from his twin sister. From that time onward, Ogo is condemned by his own act to eternally search for, but never actually find, his twin sister. This myth, which is cast in terms of mythical characters, describes what might be seen as the actual relationship that exists between the cosmological concepts of light and time.

Another mythical act of Ogo is that he is said to measure out the universe in eight billion "steps." As we noted in chapter 2, the word *step* is a likely cosmological reference to the concept of a cubit, an ancient unit of measure that is traditionally defined as the distance from a person's elbow to the tip of the middle finger, and alternately as the length of the average pace or step of a person. From the standpoint of modern astronomy, the size of the visible universe is commonly given as approximately eight billion light years, not cubits, so, considering the many other apparent relationships between the Dogon myths and science, the suggestion is that the Dogon myth establishes a symbolic equivalence between the concept of a cubit and the notion of a light year. This interpretation is supported in the Egyptian hieroglyphic language, where the word for "cubit" is given as a compound of the words *aakhu,* meaning "light," and *meh,* meaning "measure." This is also consistent with our previous observation that the word Dogon itself centers on a root that means "light."

A second apparent convention of these ancient cosmologies is found in the names of the earliest priestly tribes and is understood in terms of the Dogon word Sigi, which is the name given to an important Dogon festival of the stars of Sirius. We see this word as a likely counterpart to the ancient Egyptian word *skhai,* which means "to celebrate a festival."[8] In *The Shining Ones,* Hagan interprets the term Amazigh as combining the names of two deities: Amma (a likely Dogon counterpart to Amen in Egypt) and, from her perspective, Asar (a counterpart to the Egyptian Osiris). My own outlook on the word Amazigh is that it combines the name of the Dogon creator-god Amma with the Dogon and Egyptian word *sigi* and *skhai* to create a compound term that conveys the meaning "celebrates Amma." From this perspective, these North African tribes—in whose languages the names Amma and Amen are often equated—were seemingly named for the deity they honored, which would seem to be the same creator-god that is, even in modern times, recognized by the Dogon priests.

In our studies of the priestly Na-khi, or Na-xi, tribe of Tibet and China, we carried this observation one step further, noting that the complex suffix *khi,* or *xi,* that forms the second part of their tribal name again calls to mind the Dogon and Egyptian words *sigi* and *skhai.* We argued in *The Cosmological Origins of Myth and Symbol* that the term Na-khi, or Na-xi, combines the word *na,* a phonetic value we associate with the mother goddess Neith, with this same suffix *sigi,* or *skhai,* and so conveys the meaning of "celebrates Na, or Neith." We argued that, in traditional views of the language of the Na-khi, the term *na* reasonably conveys the notion of "mother" and that the concept of "celebrating" can also be assigned to the term *khi,* or *xi.* Realizing that important cosmological terms of the Dogon, Buddhists, and Egyptians typically carry more than one meaning, it seems significant that a second meaning for the term *na* can also be "strong." We found that this meaning is shared commonly in the languages of the Na-khi, the Dogon, and the Egyptian hieroglyphic language. However, in the language of the Na-khi alone, the word *na* can take on the additional meaning of "black." This is a designation that we proposed was derived in Tibet or China, which is consistent with the traditionally accepted belief that the Na-khi were themselves originally black Africans.

This apparent naming convention, under which very ancient tribes appear to have been named for the deity their tradition emphasized, serves as a kind of marker that implies, based on the format of the group's name alone, whether the members of a given tribe were the likely keepers of this same cosmology. By this same logic, we proposed that an ancient tribal name for the Egyptians, Mera, represents another likely expression of this same convention. The leading glyphs used to write the word Mera spell the Egyptian word for "love," while Ra is the name of the sun god who was highly revered in ancient Egyptian culture. Taken together, the glyphs of the word imply that the name could mean "loves Ra." In similar fashion, an ancient name for the tribe of the Hebrews, who are thought to have been contemporaneous with ancient Egypt, was Yahuda. Yah is the name of the Hebrew god, and *huda* means "to praise." Together, the two parts of the word convey the meaning "praises Yah."

We know based on our comparative studies that signature elements of our cosmology can be found as far distant from Egypt and Africa as Polynesia and that the native cosmology of the Maori of New Zealand defines a concept of an atom that is comparable to definitions of the *po* given in Dogon cosmology. For the Maori, this concept is couched in an esoteric tradition that is described as functioning much like the mystery tradition of the Dogon. We showed in *Sacred Symbols of the Dogon* that each deity of Egyptian culture seems to represent a discrete stage or concept of cosmology and carries a name that is a phonetic match for the appropriate cosmological term. For example, for both the Dogon and the ancient Egyptians the word *nu* represents the concept of primordial waters (Nun is the Egyptian goddess of the primordial waters), while the term *ma* seems to represent the act of perception that initiates creation by catalyzing the transformation of matter from its wavelike form to that of particles. So it may not be surprising that the term Maori can be interpreted, according to our proposed tribe-naming convention, to mean "embraces Ma."

The preceding discussion provides the background necessary to support our own view regarding the quasi-mythical or quasi-historical nature of the Chinese sovereign or Sage King named Fu-xi. Our expectation based on the naming convention just described is that the name of a Chinese tribe that is contemporaneous with ancient Egypt and that shares the same cosmology will likely reflect the stage of creation that was specifically emphasized or celebrated by that tribe. From a cosmological standpoint, the form of the name Fu-xi itself (along with the

already-discussed complications of its suffix *xi,* or *hsi*) fits the naming pattern we described. This suggests that it properly belonged to an
ancient priestly tribe, not to an individual, nor to a line of emperors or
to a deity. Moreover, we also know that some Chinese scholars equate
the name Fu-xi to the name Pau-xi, an identification that lends further
credence to our inference, since we already understand the term *po,* or
pau, to represent a recognizable stage of creation—a fundamental unit
of matter comparable to the atom. In this light, if we apply the rule of
our apparent naming convention, then the term Pau-xi, or *pau skhai,*
would seem to convey the meaning of "celebrates the po." From this
perspective, the very earliest surviving references to Fu-xi would seem
to align both the name and the concept squarely with the system of
cosmology we have defined in our previous studies.

The iconography of Fu-xi and Nu-wa and the tools they are
depicted as holding in their hands (a carpenter's square and a compass,
respectively) suggest that one of their joint functions must relate to the
measuring of the universe (figure 3.1). Some scholars argue that Fu-xi
measures "the squareness of the Earth" and Nu-wa "the roundness of the
heavens." In this way, the concept of creation in earliest China would
seem to be intimately related to the geometric squaring of a circle—the
same concept on which the plan of a stupa is overtly based. Again, we
find support for a similar view in ancient Egyptian hieroglyphic words,
where the word *aha,* which means "compass," can be interpreted symbolically to read "supports or defines circularity."[9] The likely Egyptian
correlate to Fu-xi's carpenter's square is a glyph that, in Budge's view,
represents "a corner" ⅂. We commonly find Egyptian words whose
meanings relate to rectangularity and corners (what Snodgrass refers
to as "quadrature") spelled with glyphs that we take to symbolize the
concept of earth or mass: ⌒ ⟋ ⌐. Meanwhile, the very concept of measurement in Egypt seems to be consonant with the Chinese references.
The Egyptian word *ap,* meaning "to measure," reads, according to our
symbolic method, "that which is ⟨ a space □," symbolizing, as we interpret, the concept of a space with the image of a square.[10]

If, on one level, we consider Nu-wa and Fu-xi to be the first two of the Sage Kings of China, then Yan Di of the Han dynasty (206 BCE–220 CE) would be the third. He is referred to as the Fiery Emperor. Incomplete evidence and conflicting historical accounts within the Chinese tradition make it difficult to say much with certainty about the history of the Fiery Emperor. There are conflicting claims regarding when he lived, where he was born, and what historical role he may have played. Some researchers consider him to have been a mythical, rather than a historical, character. Some scholars argue, much as we have in regard to Fu-xi, that the term Fiery Emperor refers not to an individual but rather to a group of individuals, and they attribute the conflicting histories to that view. Some believe that each successive leader of the Yan Di tribe was referred to by the name Yan Di.[11] Debate also exists

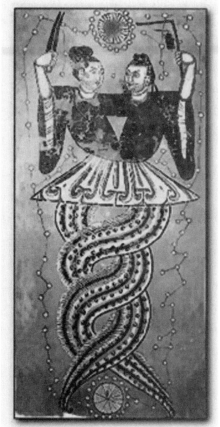

Figure 3.1. An ancient painting of Nu-wa and Fu-xi showing the two holding the tools of creation—a compass and a square

over whether the name Yan Di may actually refer to the same person as the Emperor Shennong. In any case, tradition assigns a series of specific attributes and actions to the Fiery Emperor.

First, as his name suggests, Yan Di is credited with having been in command of fire, and so he is sometimes interpreted as having been a sun deity. There are statements in the *Zuo Zhuan*, or *Zhuangzi*—one of the earliest written works of Chinese history that bears the name of the philosopher who wrote it—that attest that in 525 BCE the descendants of Yan Di were recognized as having long been masters of fire and having used the symbol for fire in their names.[12] Likewise, it is said that Yan Di was born weak, that his head developed skin boils, and that he spent his life in search of herbal medicines as remedies for disease—one of which ultimately poisoned and killed him. Again like the mythical ancestors who were said to have introduced the eight cultivated grains of Dogon agriculture, Yan Di, through his identity with Shennong, is credited with having brought cultivatable grains to China, and so he is also associated with the same civilizing skills of agriculture that we associate with our plan of cosmology. Some linguists translate the name Shennong as a compound term that means "god of farming" or "god of grains." Significantly, the use of compound terms represents one of the consistent attributes of our ancient plan of cosmology.

One observation that comes out of our studies in cosmology is that the further back in time we go, the more apparent commonality in language we seem to observe between cultures. Also, because cosmology seems to have preceded the advent of written language in most cultures, any relationships that originally existed between cosmological words would be reflected not in the common spelling of words, but rather—as the Dogon priests assert—in common pronunciation. Given this, it appears that we can positively link legends of the Fiery Emperor in China to our cosmological tradition of knowledgeable ancestors through a series of word comparisons, once again made against Budge's *An Egyptian Hieroglyphic Dictionary*.

As we explore this possibility, the first thing we notice is that the term for a group of ancestor-gods in Egypt, *akeru,* is based on the pho-netic root *ak,* meaning "to become weak," an attribute that is assigned in China to the Fiery Emperor.[13] The same is true for the Egyptian word *aku-t,* which means "boils."[14] A little additional research shows that other proclaimed traits or actions of the Fiery Emperor also take expression in the Egyptian hieroglyphic language in direct relation to an Egyptian root word that means "ancestors." Dictionary entries for the Egyptian word *pa* refer to the concept of an ancestor and to the concept of fire, and it is the root of the word *paat-t,* which refers to "woods or barks used in medicine," comparable to the herbal remedies of Yan Di. The word *pa-t,* which is defined by Budge as "a kind of farm land," is also based on this same root.[15] These word meanings all reflect attributes that are specifically associated with the Fiery Emperor in China, who is treated as a revered ancestor. This observation suggests that the tradi-tional Chinese stories relating to the Fiery Emperor may have constituted a kind of mask for a set of related cosmological terms and thereby reflect a use of multiple meanings, homonyms, or wordplay from Chinese cos-mology. This in turn suggests that these same terms in China may have taken the same basic form as they did in ancient Egypt and so reflect the same sets of interrelated meanings. If so, then the implication is that the terms themselves came out of closely matching cosmological plans.

The next of the Sage Kings of ancient China was the Yellow Emperor, who was also called Huangdi or Huangti. The term *huang,* meaning "yellow," was a homonym for the word *huang,* meaning "august." It is surmised that one glyph may have been deliberately substituted for the other when the term for "august" became taboo in China due to political infighting, which thus altered both the meaning of the word and the designation of the emperor.[16] Like the ancestor-teachers of the Dogon, the Yellow Emperor was credited with having brought specific civilizing skills to the Chinese people. He was respon-sible for having introduced the concept of proper clothing to China, a concept that the Dogon specifically attribute to the civilizing plan of their ancestor-teachers. He was also said to have invented the drum, an instrument that plays an important symbolic role in the civilizing plan and cosmology of the Dogon ancestors.

In addition, there are tales that date from 220 BCE of the Chinese emperor Qin's discovery of an ancient shrine on a mountaintop that honored the Yellow Emperor. This shrine clearly memorialized an ancestral emperor long prior to Qin and so contradicted Qin's own parochial view, in which he cast himself in the role of "First Emperor" of China. As a consequence of his discovery, Qin ultimately chose to set aside his own claim and honor the Yellow Emperor, which he did by making offerings and paying tribute to acknowledge his ancient predecessor.[17] Once again, when we turn to an examination of comparative language, we see that the multiple meanings of cosmological terms as they are understood in other cultures seem to offer a coherent explanation for this tradition in China. In this case we notice that in the Egyptian hieroglyphic language, the word for "yellow" is formed from a root that can also mean "to pay homage."

Moving beyond our discussion of the likeliest candidates to fill the role of the Three Sage Kings in China, there seems to be consensus among scholars that the first of the Five Virtuous Emperors would be the emperor Yao. He is traditionally described as a respected leader who traveled the countryside and won the loyalty of the general public through his willingness to seek counsel—both by way of his talent for choosing well-selected advisors and through the way in which he proactively sought constructive suggestions from the common people. The legend is that he lived at a time when ten suns shone in the sky and during a period of great heat and drought that became ruinous to much of the vegetation on the planet. Yao ordered an archer named Yi (or Houyi) to shoot nine of the ten suns from their place in the sky. By so doing, he succeeded in returning the seasonal temperatures to normal. Soon after this, the land was visited with great floods that persisted despite Yao's determined efforts. Yao appointed a talented subordinate named Gun to solve the flooding problem, but after nine unsuccessful years of determined effort on the part of Gun, Yao ultimately sentenced him to death for his inability to stem the floods. The rendering of this punishment was perceived by the public as being unjust, and Yao was greatly criticized for having imposed it.[18]

One rationale that potentially explains many of these mythic attributes of Emperor Yao is again found linguistically in relation to words found in Budge's *An Egyptian Hieroglyphic Dictionary*. These words center on the phonemes *u* and *ua,* which in our view are likely Egyptian correlates to the Chinese name Yao. Budge tells us that just as Yao was characterized as a traveler, the Egyptian word *ua* can mean "to go away, to be remote or afar," while the word *uaiu* refers to remote travelers. The term *ua-t neter* refers to a deified traveler who is on the road. Just as Yao is remembered as a ruler who actively sought good counsel, so the Egyptian word *uaa* means "to think, to meditate, to take counsel" and can refer to a "king who communed with his heart." Consonant with the idea that Yao lived in a time of scorching weather, yet another word entry, *ua,* means "to burn, to be hot." And as tradition describes a period of inundation during Yao's reign, the Egyptian phrase *ua en ater* refers to a river flood. Chinese tradition tells us that Yao was criticized for his treatment of Gun's failure to stem the flooding. A similar meaning is conveyed by the Egyptian word *ua,* which means "to speak evil of someone," and the Egyptian term *uaua,* which means "to curse the king." In short, as unlikely as it may seem, each of the mythical attributes traditionally assigned to Emperor Yao appear to be once again reflected in Egyptian words that take their phonetic roots from homonyms for the emperor's name.[19]

If we take this unorthodox analysis one step further, we find that some additional synchronicities can be seen to exist between the myth of Yao and the meanings of related words of cosmology. As we have already noted, the Chinese concept of the ten suns and the symbolic form of the two-glyph word used to express it align well with the word *met,* which, by our reading, defines the ancient Egyptian ten-day week. Words for the concept of a week were written with two glyphs in both cultures: the sun glyph ☉ and the glyph for the number ten ∩. Because the sun glyph can represent the concept of a day or the concept of the sun in both cultures, either could be reasonably interpreted as referring to "ten suns." Budge defines a homonym for this same word *met* in Egypt that means "inundation," which is yet another concept associated with Yao in China.[20] The Egyptian word *pestch,* meaning "nine," is based on the same phonetic root as *pesh-t,* which refers to the "bending or stringing of an archer's bow," and so, within the context of our cosmology, it could serve to symbolically connect the notion of an archer to the concept of nine suns.[21]

Furthermore, there is an alternate tradition in China that treats the nine mythical suns that were shot from the sky as if they were birds. A related Egyptian concept, *pestch-ti,* which refers to nine gods, is expressed in terms of a bird glyph . In other words, there is a perspective from which the history of Yao that describes the mythical existence of ten suns, the archer who shoots nine of the suns, and the following inundation can be seen as yet another example in which the diverse meanings of two important cosmological terms appear to have been woven into a single, publicly repeated mythological storyline. In this way, the multiple word meanings (which for the Dogon represent esoteric knowledge to be safeguarded by priests) seem to have been carried down through the generations in China by an unknowing public, safeguarded in the storylines of popular myths or folktales. Here, in their fairytale-like aspect, the esoteric cosmological references were still effectively disguised from unknowing eyes, effectively hidden in plain view as a series of mythical traits and actions assigned to a beloved Chinese emperor.

Our method of cross-cultural linguistic analysis for shared terms of cosmology may also apply to the next likely candidate in our series of Virtuous Emperors, whose name was Shun. Attributes traditionally applied to Shun in ancient China again seem to relate to ancient Egyptian word meanings that center on the phoneme *sh* or *sha.* (We should note that it remains uncertain how any given ancient Egypt glyph may have actually been pronounced, and so the values Budge cites should be regarded as only tentative.) We are told that Shun was nominated by Emperor Yao to be a government official. Budge's dictionary tells us that the word *sha* means "to appoint." We are told that Shun lived to be a hundred years old. Again reflecting the Chinese meaning, Budge tells us that the Egyptian word *sha-t* means "a hundred."[22] From China we learn that whenever Shun made an effort to fish or farm, his neighbors would always take care that the most fertile piece of land or productive body of water was made available to him. For Budge, the word *shaasha* means "reverence or respect," while Shai was the name of an Egyptian god of luck.[23] Clearly some of the Chinese/Egyptian word comparisons are inexact, yet the resemblances would seem to go beyond simple coincidence.

On another level, the story of Yao and Shun and their efforts to stem an inundation follows the contours of the early stages in the creation of matter as they are given in other cosmologies. Two passages from book three of the *Zhuangzi* describe the world as having been rendered chaotic by vast waters and tell of how order was reestablished by Yao, Shun, and their deputy Yu, who employed fire as a kind of remedy. The concurrence of these familiar cosmological themes and images in their expected sequence suggests that the histories of these emperors might well be interpreted as allegorical remnants of an earlier, perhaps more comprehensive narrative of creation similar to the one given by the Dogon priests.[24] Norman J. Girardot cites Chang Kwang-chih's classification of the traditional sequence of cosmological events to support the idea that the mythical Chinese ancestors, from Nu-wa and Fu-xi through Yao, Shun, and Yu, belong to the periods of cosmological creation associated with the concept of hundun.[25]

The next of the Virtuous Emperors is Tang, the founder of the Shang dynasty. He is the first of the mythical ancestors whose historical existence is overtly supported by tangible evidence. Nonetheless, there are aspects to his life that could still be interpreted as the continuation of a cosmological narrative that relates to the formation of matter. In the well-explicated sequence of events that define the stages of matter in the Dogon/Egyptian tradition, a watery chaos, symbolized by waves, is disrupted by an act of perception, symbolized by fire. This disruption causes the waves of water to raise up, grow, and separate, and thereby establishes within the universe a principle of duality. One of the memorable acts of Tang in Chinese mythological history that might be seen to parallel these events is that he recognizes the talents of a subordinate named Yin Yi and promotes him (raises him up) from the level of a servant to that of prime minister. Although on one level Yin Yi is deemed to have been a historical minister of Tang, the story of his birth is given in mythological terms that relate to a spring of water. A spring is a natural feature that also facilitates the "raising up" of water. Tang is also credited with having founded two capital cities of the Shang dynasty, whose artifacts have been explored by Chinese archaeologists, an attributed accomplishment that, along with his choice to promote a subordinate, might be seen as an expression of the principle of duality.

The first enthroned emperor of the Western Zhou dynasty (1046 BCE–771 BCE) was King Wu, but he is traditionally grouped together with his father, whose honorary title, King Wen, was bestowed on him posthumously by his son. Then, after only a single year on the throne, King Wu himself died and was succeeded by his thirteen-year-old son, King Cheng. The elder grandfather, King Wen, had long plotted to overthrow the Shang dynasty but was ultimately frustrated in that desire. Instead, it is said that he was imprisoned for the last seven years of his life, time that he used to research the eight trigrams of the *I Ching* and create the *Book of Changes,* in which they are described.

Once again, the events of the lives of these kings might be seen to describe the next logical steps in the formation of matter, based on our cosmological model. From the perspective of the Dogon creation tradition, after a primordial wave is perceived, it is raised up like a tent or a hill, separates, and becomes dual. From there, it passes through a series of seven spiraling vibrations that transform it into the egg of the world, referred to as the *po pilu.* The Dogon define this egg as a fundamental component of matter similar to the Calabi-Yau space in string theory. The one-year reign of King Wu and his subsequent death, which ushers in the reign of King Cheng, stands symbolically at the eighth stage of vibration of the egg. This is the point at which the seventh vibration is said to rupture the egg—the stage that simultaneously completes the first egg and initiates a new second egg.

Supportive of this interpretation is a significant sequence of numbers relating to the *I Ching* method of divination, as described in the *Book of Changes,* which are, in fact, attributed to King Wen. When graphed, these numbers produce a mandala that is recognizable as the E8 shape—a geometric figure that provides string theorists with a mathematical basis for the Calabi-Yau space (figure 3.2).

Figure 3.2. Mandala-shaped graph of I Ching *numbers*

As we have noted, the ancestor-teachers of the Dogon tradition are credited with having introduced, hand in hand with their cosmology, a defined set of civilizing concepts and skills. These are arguably the same concepts and skills that would be required to transform a society of hunter-gatherers into an agrarian society. They include the introduction of the concept of clothing, the ability to spin and weave thread, and the ability to plow a field, plant, cultivate, store seeds, and harvest a crop. They also include basic skills of metallurgy necessary to fashion the tools and implements of agriculture. They would also necessarily include the ability to accurately measure time and to forecast seasons. According to the Dogon priests, they include knowledge of the art of pottery and the ability to produce clay pots necessary for the storage of grain before it is planted and after it has been grown and harvested. We see many of these same concepts and skills attributed to the mythical Chinese counterparts of these ancestor-teachers.

4
THE CHINESE CONCEPT OF THE MULBERRY TREE

In China, the mythological tale of the ten suns and the archer Yi who shoots down nine of the suns is also a source for the mythological concept of the mulberry tree. Although this is not a theme that has been well explicated in the other cosmologies we have studied, evidence of such a concept is widely found in other traditions. In fact, Adrian Snodgrass refers to "the ubiquitous tradition [of a world tree] whose branches support the rising sun, symbolized by an animal, bird or fruit" in *The Symbolism of the Stupa*.[1] From a mythological standpoint, the symbolism of the mulberry tree bears similarities to—but is distinct from—the tree of life symbolism that is commonly associated with the concept of the axis mundi.

In China, the mulberry tree, or *fu sang,* is somewhat obliquely defined as a kind of "spirit tree" from which the "suns go out," or that somehow provided "support" for the suns. The tree was said to reach down into the watery underworld or to originate in a whirlpool of water that was described as residing at the foot of the tree. In China, it is alternately called the *fu mu,* a term that immediately calls to mind the Egyptian word *mu,* which is sometimes seen as a counterpart to the Dogon concept of *nu* in references to the primordial waters.[2] In China, perhaps the most explicit description of the mulberry tree mythos comes

57

out of the *Shanhaijing,* an early Chinese compilation of myths and geological references. There it is described as rising above a pool of swirling water in the Tang Valley, where the ten suns "bathe." In the Egyptian hieroglyphic language, the word *bathe,* which Budge pronounces "aa" or "aai," can be interpreted symbolically to mean "that which ⌡ initiates ⌐ from waves or water 〰 the growth of ⌘ particles ⌐, followed by three vertical lines |||—the plural determinative."*[3]

The nine suns are said to perch on the tree's lower branches, and the one sun—the sun that ultimately survives the arrows of the archer Yi—sits on its top branch. Another description of the tree from the *Shanhaijing* suggests that when one sun reached the tree, another sun went out. This again calls to mind the spiraling divisions of the Dogon egg of the world, which is characterized as a series of sun-like rays, where the eighth stage that completes and then pierces the first egg also initiates a second egg.

Snodgrass also tells us that, in Buddhism, this world tree is associated with the concept of Surya, the sun, whose leg or foot "ascends the vault and upholds the sky." This leg is conceived of as having three segments, identified respectively as heaven, midspace, and Earth.[4] Buddhist symbolism defines these three divisions in terms that could be comparable to the three worlds of matter conceptualized in the Dogon creation tradition: the First World, in which perfectly ordered matter exists in wavelike form; the Second World (comparable to the Egyptian underworld), where the concept of disorder is introduced and matter is fundamentally reordered; and the Third World that we perceive on Earth. These commonalities with the Dogon creation tradition suggest that the mulberry tree plays a role within the world of matter (the microcosm) that is comparable to the one played by the axis mundi within the larger universe (the macrocosm).

The concept of a mulberry tree is expressed by two words in the

---

*A determinative is a glyph that is added to a hieroglyphic word in order to clarify its context, meaning, or tense. For example, the name of an Egyptian deity or deified concept might be followed by the god or goddess glyph.

Egyptian hieroglyphic language. A symbolic reading of each word entry suggests that their meanings relate to how the bending or warping force of gravity causes waves to evolve in the shape of a spiral that is responsible for the formation of mass. This spiral would be comparable to the one associated with the Dogon egg of the world. However, if we apply our symbolic method of reading Egyptian hieroglyphs, it becomes clear that the first of these words, pronounced "merit," meets our criteria for a defining word—a word whose glyphs symbolically define a concept that is to be associated with its unpronounced trailing glyph.* In this case, the trailing glyph consists of the figure of a tree 〈 that is overlaid with the figure of a branch ⤳, and so it might reasonably convey the symbolic meaning of "branch of a tree." This image, which agrees with statements given within the Chinese myths themselves, leads us to think that one purpose of the mythical concept of the mulberry tree might be to draw our attention to the branches themselves. This same conclusion could be inferred from the Chinese symbolism, if we simply ask ourselves what the three alternate symbolic images of berries, birds, and suns have in common with one another in relation to the mulberry tree. One immediate answer is that berries grow on branches, birds land and sit on branches, and the sun shines on the leaves of the branches. Each symbolic image would again seem to draw our attention to the branches of the tree.

Egyptian words for "branch" are written with symbols that we associate with the processes of the formation of matter. These include the image of a fish ⤳, which we interpret within Dogon cosmology to symbolize the processes by which waves come to be transformed into mass or matter following an act of perception. These symbols include the spiral shape ℰ, which in the Dogon creation tradition is understood to inscribe the endpoints of the egg's seven rays, which are said to be of increasing length. It is by way of this symbolism that the shape of the

---

*Some Egyptian words include one or more final glyphs that function like silent letters in English. Our view is that the leading glyphs of these word reflect concepts that assign symbolic meanings to these trailing glyphs.

spiral comes to characterize the egg of the world. The symbols include the hemisphere glyph ⌒, which we take to symbolize mass or matter, and they also include the Egyptian three-stemmed plant glyph, which, in our view, symbolizes the tree of life and the three worlds of matter.

There is only one variety of mulberry tree that is native to China—the white mulberry, or *Morus alba*. Figure 4.1 gives an example of the configuration of the branches of a similar mulberry tree. We see that the tree consists of branches that spread out from a central stem, with individual berries—often in pairs—that are situated centrally at intervals along the branch.

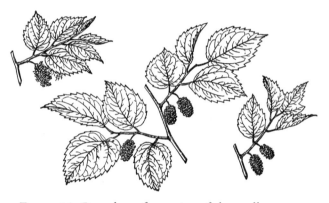

Figure 4.1. Branch configuration of the mulberry tree

If we follow the linguistic and mythic hints given in the Chinese mulberry tree myth that seem to relate to the formation of matter and explore the scientific concept of branches as it relates to string theory, the immediate idea that presents itself is the concept of the fundamental lemma. This is a belief drawn from number theory, which holds that any system that can be derived mathematically rests on a foundational theorem. Although this seems like a relatively straightforward concept, it is one that actually took several decades to positively demonstrate through mathematical proof.

One of the simplest examples of a mathematical concept that can be expressed in terms of a fundamental lemma is the act of counting from one to ten. The Chinese myth of the ten suns, in which the archer Yi is said to shoot nine of the suns from the sky, leaving only the tenth, can be seen as a way of illustrating symbolically within the narrative of a mythic storyline the concept of counting from one to ten.

The idea that the mythic concept of the mulberry tree likely relates to the concept of the fundamental lemma of string theory gains support when we look to string theory diagrams that relate to its fundamental lemma. The graph in figure 4.2 is based on the fundamental lemma of string theory. It defines a branching structure that is similar in many ways to the branches of the mulberry tree.

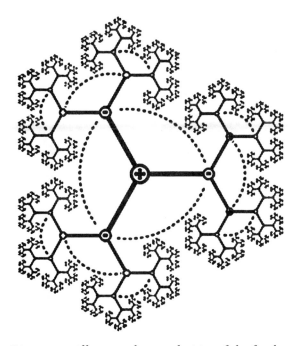

Figure 4.2. Diagram to illustrate the complexities of the fundamental lemma of string theory (from William A. Casselman, the Institute for Advanced Study)

In string theory, formulas are used to define how matter will behave in its wavelike form, to predict the likely attributes of the Calabi-Yau space, to calculate the sizes and masses of various fundamental particles, and to extrapolate how matter then emerges from its various component elements. In other words, just as the mulberry tree symbolism states, the concept of the fundamental lemma applies to the First World of matter as waves, to the Second World of the Calabi-Yau space, and to the Third World of matter as we perceive it. Ultimately, these structures uphold and support the concept of time, a concept that is symbolized in the written languages of various cultures by the sun glyph.

If we imagine an ancient teacher looking for an object in nature to symbolize the complex concept of the fundamental lemma of matter, the branch of the mulberry tree seems like a fairly inspired choice to convey that concept in diagrammatic form. Furthermore, we can see from figure 4.3 that the leaves of the mulberry tree can sometimes take

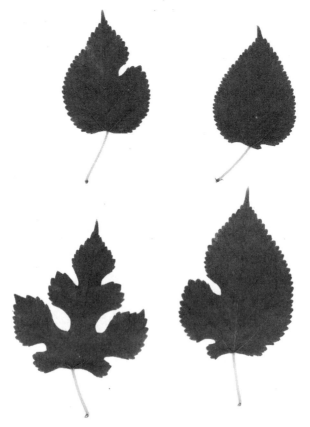

Figure 4.3. The mulberry tree leaves on the top left and bottom right (seen horizontally) seem to take the shape of a stylized profile of a bird.

the shape of a stylized profile of birds (see the leaves on the top left and bottom right, viewed horizontally). Meanwhile, the round, unopened buds of the white mulberry tree present an image that calls to mind the Chinese and Egyptian sun glyph itself.

The Dogon priests describe a mythical tree that appears in the very earliest stages of creation, whose fruit, like the unripe fruit of the mulberry, can be poisonous. For this reason, the tree is considered to be "the enemy of water" because it produces leaves and fruit that "appear only after the rain," implying that its growth does not actually assist the processes of creation. The small branches of the tree are treated as unwanted foliage that must be trimmed in order for the tree to grow.[5]

5
THE WELL-FIELD SYSTEM

The well-field system was an ancient method of distributing cultivated land. Although this system has recognizable roots in ancient cosmology, it is not a concept that we have previously explored in the books of this series. As a generic concept, the well-field system defined a square that enclosed nine smaller square plots of land, organized as eight outer plots that surrounded a ninth inner one. Typically, each outer plot was assigned to a family for cultivation, while the ninth was reserved either for some common use, such as the placement of a shared well (as the term *well-field* implies) or smithy's forge, or for the tithed benefit of a local landowner or official.

In the Dogon culture, this fundamental unit of land was said to symbolize the primal field—a configuration that celebrated the descent of a mythical ark or granary, within which the seeds of the eight cultivated grains were originally housed.[1] As was true for the Dogon granary itself, the concept of the primal field was conceptualized on two separate levels: one that was strictly symbolic or theoretic in nature, and one that was meant for practical application as a part of the everyday life of the Dogon tribe.

In the first case, the concept of the Dogon primal field was treated as an extension of their cosmology and existed only as a theoretic construct. The individual squares that composed the field were of irregular measurement, were aligned to the cardinal points, and were laid out in the form of a spiral whose shape mimicked the spiraling evolution of space as it was described during the formation of matter. The act of plowing a field was equated to the act of weaving a cloth; the Dogon priests say that, originally, both civilizing skills—weaving and plowing—were carried out according to the same method, which itself was said to mirror a process of creation. According to this metaphoric conception, the Dogon system described an agricultural field that was cultivated in squares and that, in its totality, gave the impression of a woven coverlet or blanket.

One Dogon family would take possession of one of the eight plots, one associated with each of the eight grains of Dogon agriculture.[2] In actual practice, the concept of the well-field involved nine squares of land that, in contrast to the irregular sizes of the theoretical construct, each measured exactly eight cubits per side—the same dimensions as are specified by the Dogon priests for the square flat roof of the symbolic granary. This common dimension underscores the view of the Dogon priests that the granary roof was intended on one level to define a fundamental unit of land. As such, the matched dimensions also uphold our view that the squared roof of the granary was an original feature of an ancient cosmological plan that seems to have been adapted at some later point to produce the alternate-squared base of a Buddhist stupa, whose dimensions—representing a larger square—typically could not be in agreement with the well-field land units.

According to the Dogon priests, the recurrence of the number eight in various aspects of Dogon agricultural life was meant to symbolize the eight stages of vibration through which the threads of matter were said to pass during the evolution of the egg of the world described in the Dogon creation tradition. In *The Science of the Dogon,* I compared these vibrations to the vibrations of the primordial threads that modern astrophysicists associate with the Calabi-Yau space in string theory.

In actual practice, in the Dogon agricultural system described by

Marcel Griaule, the outer eight squares of the primal field were allotted for cultivation by Dogon families, while a ninth square—situated on the north side of the plot—was reserved to house the forge of a smithy, whose job it was to fashion the metal implements of agriculture that were required for cultivation of the fields. Dogon tribal rules that governed divisions of labor within the tribe strictly prohibited the smith from actually participating in the processes of cultivation but required those who farmed the outer fields to share a portion of their crop with him at the time of the harvest.[3] According to one description given by Marcel Griaule, the squares of cultivated farmland on the plain, when viewed from a high observation point, gave the overall impression of a checkerboard.[4]

Hints of a similar set of related concepts can be found in ancient Egyptian words that express the concepts defined by the Dogon priests. For example, in Egypt we find the concept of a "well of water," given as *am* or *amam,* expressed in terms of the phonetic root *am,* which can also refer to a "weaving instrument or loom." Since we know the well occupied the central square of the nine-square well-field plot, the phonetic root of the word suggests that it takes on the same symbolic aspect as Amma's place at the central point of the egg-in-a-ball figure. From this perspective, the well-field plot can be seen as a squared version of the round egg-in-a-ball figure, and so brings us back again to the cosmological theme of the squaring of a circle. This same phonetic root *am* also forms the basis of the word *amam-t,* which refers to a "parcel of land."[5]

In similar fashion, we find an Egyptian word *henb,* meaning "to allot land by measure," which is based on the same phonetic root as the term *henbi,* meaning "well or spring," and so suggests that, in Egypt, the concept of land measure was linked to the idea of a well.[6] In accordance with the Dogon practice, we know that parcels of land in Egypt were set out using the cubit as a unit of measure and were aligned to the cardinal points based on a central gnomon and the sun—the same essential process that is known to have been employed in the alignment of a Buddhist stupa.[7] Egyptian hieroglyphic words also reflect meanings that are comparable to the Dogon symbolism that characterizes these squares of cultivated land to a coverlet or blanket. In Budge's dictionary we find two entries for the word *aft*. The first refers to "a rectangular plot of land," and the second, given with the same pronunciation, to the concept of the "coverlet of a bed."[8] The concurrence of these meanings attached to words that are homonyms of one another suggests the existence of symbolism in Egypt that again matches that of the Dogon.

As we have seen with other concepts of ancient Chinese cosmology, a longstanding controversy exists among scholars over the precise nature of the well-field system as it may or may not have been practiced in ancient China. This rigorous system of land distribution is described in the *Mencius,* which is a collection of legends and myths attributed to an early Chinese philosopher of the same name. The technique was said to have produced a patchwork of cultivated fields similar to those described by the Dogon, which, when viewed from a distance, gave the overall appearance of a checkerboard. Under this system, some Chinese researchers believe that eight families each worked their own plots of land. These were joined together around a central plot like the squares of the Dogon primal field. The central plot may have belonged to a local lord or dignitary, and the responsibility for working this plot may have been assigned to these same peasant families, while the produce it yielded may have constituted a tax levied by the lord, who received it from the peasant families who worked the land.

In describing the system, Mencius used the imperative mood, "Please let there be . . . ," and so cannot be definitively said to have made an actual claim for the historical existence of the system.[9] In part because of this, some scholars doubt that such a rigorous system of land distribution could have been set in place in antiquity and argue that the system may have existed simply as an idealized concept, similar to the aspect of the primal field concept of the Dogon that is described as having been symbolic. Other scholars accept the system as an actual agricultural practice that, according to tradition, was implemented by the early Chinese sages. They argue that just such a system has survived among some minority groups in China, a fact that could reflect the actuality of its existence in ancient times. The Chinese term for this system of agriculture—the well field—implies by its very name that nine cultivated units shared a common well of water.[10]

Adrian Snodgrass, in his seminal work *Architecture, Time, and Eternity,* affirms his belief in the historical existence of a well-field system in ancient China as related by Mencius. The system is attributed in myth to Emperor Yu and represents just one aspect of a larger world plan that was also founded on divisions of nine. This plan is set forth in the "Treatise on Topography" and is consistent with the Tsou Yen school of cosmology. It is in this same treatise that expression is given to the symbolic concept that associates the figure of a circle with heaven and that of a square with Earth. Some researchers attribute the impulse to conceptualize Chinese cosmology in terms of squares to these references.[11] From the perspective of this topological plan, the world, as representative of the largest land unit, was described as having nine continents, with Asia, the continent on which China resides, at the conceptual center.[12]

This scheme extended geographically downward to a plan for China itself, which was divided into eight outer provinces that surrounded a ninth royal province at the center. Snodgrass says that the plan involved descending units of nine that dictated the original conceptual layout for the earliest Chinese cities, palaces, temples, and houses, all of which were conceived on the basis of nine squares. These, like the nine Dogon agricultural plots, were aligned to the cardinal points. According to Snodgrass, it seems only sensible that this concept was ultimately also reflected in the basic agricultural unit of eight farm plots organized around a ninth central plot where a common well of water was located (figure 5.1). Snodgrass affirms that the outer plots were assigned to eight families, each of whom farmed their own plot, with the food that they harvested for their own benefit. Together, the families also shared responsibility for cultivating the central plot, whose produce was given as a tax to a central administrator. Snodgrass perceives these divisions of nine as having been an expression of the fundamental ordering of space within a system of cosmology that was similar to the plan defined by the base plan of a Buddhist stupa, and so it serves as yet another symbolic connection to the Dogon. He tells us that the Chinese ideogram *jing,* or *ching,* which means "well," takes a form similar to the modern pound sign ♯ and is, itself, a drawn representation of the well-field plan. The Chinese word for "well field," *jing tian,* is written with two glyphs as ♯田.[13]

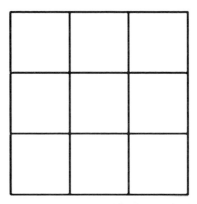

Figure 5.1. The basic unit of the well-field plan consisted of eight farm plots organized around a ninth central plot with a common well. These plots also formed a nine-square mandala.

We know with certainty that an organizational plan for China in the divisions of nine as Snodgrass describes it was historically implemented on at least some levels. We can see evidence that this plan tangibly existed in the layout of ancient Chinese cities and in their palaces and temples. Whatever authority imposed this organizational scheme on the provinces of China would almost surely also have been capable of influencing the organization of farmland among the peasants in the countryside.

Although it is entirely conceivable that distant cultures might have independently evolved methods of land allocation similar to the Dogon primal field and the Chinese well-field system, we would argue that the symbolism and terminology that are attached to these systems suggest a common origin, one that we would attribute, based on our knowledge of the Dogon model, to a shared cosmology. For instance, we consider the imperative to align ritual structures to the cardinal points to be an effective signature of the cosmologies we have studied. It arises out of concepts and principles that are carefully developed within the cosmology. Directional alignment is not an intuitive feature that would necessarily go hand in hand with the simple impulse to place nine plots of land into a square arrangement. Second, the plots of land are set out in both cases using cubits, a unit of measure that arguably originated with and signals the influence of our cosmological plan. Third, cultivated land is described metaphorically in both systems using the matched terms of *checkerboard* and *coverlet*. The assignment of multiple meanings of this style to an important concept or term is also a signature of our civilizing plan. It is our contention that these broad commonalities point to an origin within the context of a shared system of cosmology.

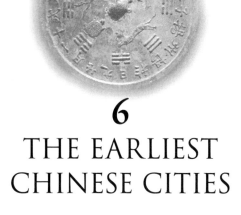

6

THE EARLIEST
CHINESE CITIES

As we approach the concept of civic centers or cities in ancient China, we are again faced with a body of evidence on which to base our findings that is, at best, inconclusive. This problem is exacerbated by the fact that many of the primary sources on which historical insights are based were typically not set down in written form until many centuries after the actual events occurred. For example, texts from late in the Shang dynasty that provide us with descriptions of what cities may have been like in the early Shang dynasty were not written until long after these cities were actually founded. Likewise, much of the graphic evidence in China that would be contemporaneous with the earliest artifacts in ancient Egypt simply failed to survive. This means that the prevailing academic opinion must often rely on reconstructed models that may represent, at best, informed guesses. Perhaps because of these types of difficulties, we again find competing schools of thought among academic researchers in regard to what the true evolution of the urban form may have actually been in China.

Although evidence for settlements in China dates from as early as 5000 BCE, the earliest significant settlements date from a period that is roughly contemporaneous with dynastic Egypt.[1] Most researchers agree that early castle-like communities emerged in China at about the same time as they did in other ancient cultures, appearing first during the era between 3000 and 2000 BCE. Evidence for the establishment of actual cities in the modern sense of the word is not apparent until the Zhou dynasty, almost a thousand years later.[2]

These early cities were characterized by several different features that could suggest the influence of our cosmology. Paul Wheatley remarks in *The Pivot of the Four Quarters* that the majority of the great capitals of Asia share the symbolic features of cardinal orientation and cardinal axiality. Likewise, it is his opinion that all the great cultures of Asia shared similar outlooks on the cosmological orientation of space, without regard to the specific tradition through which these views were filtered.[3] In China, Wheatley says, cities were traditionally aligned to the cardinal points using a method that is already familiar to us from our discussions of the Buddhist stupa. Furthermore, he tells us that this same method was also applied to the alignment of cities in ancient India. In regard to the alignment of cities in India, he writes of the initiates who implemented the alignment, "They erected a post, took the plumb-line to it [to ensure its verticality], and then observed its shadow. They described a circle, and recorded the shadow of the sun at its rising and setting."[4]

As with the alignment of a stupa, the initiates recorded the positions of these shadows at the points at which they intersected the circle, then created a line that was oriented along an east-west axis. From there, the geometry of alignment progressed with the addition of two more intersecting circles, each described around one of the first two points. These circles intersected at two points that served as the endpoints of a second line, this time oriented along a north-south axis. I argued in *The Cosmological Origins of Myth and Symbol* that the boundaries of this geometry defined a figure that has come to be known as the fish.[5] Wheatley confirms my observation in his discussion of this same geometry as it was applied to alignments in India when he states that the two intersecting points that define the north-south line are referred to as the head and tail of the fish (figure 6.1).[6]

Wheatley notes that there are instances in which the alignment of

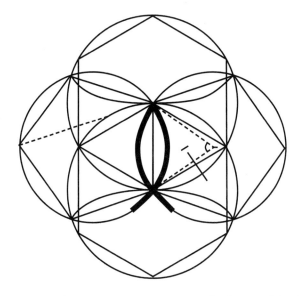

Figure 6.1. Alignment geometry creates the figure of the fish.

an ancient Chinese city deviated somewhat (anywhere from a few minutes to up to a few degrees) from true north. He largely attributes these differences to errors in methodology, to the use of sighting methods that were dependent on the location of pole stars that later moved due to the slow wobble of precession, or to conditions such as local variations in the magnetic field. Wheatley tells us that the ancient city of Glak-djang exhibits an orientation that is almost four degrees west of true north as we measure it today.[7]

Wheatley also tells us that the topography of the land apparently sometimes caused the planners of ancient Chinese cities to take significant liberties with their idealized orientation to the cardinal points. He cites the city of Hang Chou as the best example of this type of accommodation to geography. However, he states that even in the worst cases, it can be seen that efforts were still made to approximate a kind of symbolic alignment to the cardinal points.

In chapter 5, we made reference to Adrian Snodgrass's belief in an ancient organizational plan for China that was expressed in descending divisions of nine and culminated at the lowest level in well-field agricultural plots. Wheatley says that this plan, which he also associates with the well-field system, reflected an ancient mode of thought that was characterized by the symbolist poet Rene Berthelot as having been—like our cosmology—fundamentally astrobiological in nature.[8] The descending levels of this plan included a base concept for the ideal organization of the Chinese city. A belief similar to Wheatley's was expressed by Sir Thomas Browne, a seventeenth-century contemporary of Sir Francis Bacon who wrote on diverse topics of science. Browne's outlook was later put forth in a letter by Samuel Taylor Coleridge, who wrote:

> So Chinese cosmographers of the Han and later eras regarded the simple nonary square as the basis of proper order in practically every realm of space. This form was at least as important and ubiquitous in premodern Chinese cosmography as the circle was in Greek, medieval European, and Islamic cosmography.[9]

While it is tempting to imagine that the concept of divisions of nine would have consistently played out in the plan of ancient Chinese cities in ways that directly mirror the well-field system (as they seem to have done in ancient India), with eight squares laid out around a central ninth square, we find that this is not always the case. The plans of some Chinese cities appear to have been conceived instead around sixteen squares, with twelve squares surrounding four squares that, together, fulfilled the role of "center." These squares were perhaps conceptually comparable to the four elemental divisions of the Dogon egg in a ball, which the Dogon depict as four quarters of a circle. Wheatley tells us that the reason for this difference in layout—involving nine versus sixteen squares—is not readily apparent.[10]

As I noted in *The Cosmological Origins of Myth and Symbol*, it is Wheatley's belief, based on opinions expressed by Walter Fairservis of Vassar College, that the earliest civic centers in China grew up not around centers of commerce or agriculture, but rather around ritual centers. Fairservis equates these to ancient ritual centers that have been found and excavated in India, which he says functioned in much the same way as contemporaneous ceremonial centers in the Old Kingdom of ancient Egypt. Through his research, Fairservis traced a progression of development that positively links the earliest villages in India to these later known centers of ritual and ceremony.[11]

Wheatley tells us that, symbolically, the ancient Chinese city was also defined in terms of the cosmological concept of the axis mundi. This symbolism dictated the placement of important buildings such as palaces, whose location was linked conceptually to the pole star.[12] The *Kao Gong Ji* (a classic work on science and technology in ancient China) includes a description of the ideal alignments that should be reflected within the capital city of China. The city was oriented according to a pair of axes, and it was stated that the palace, which was the ruler's residence and place of administration, should be located at the intersection of these two axes, at a point referred to as the center point, or *zhong*. These two axes were associated symbolically with the axis mundi.[13]

According to Adrian Snodgrass, the two lines that represent these axes also define the four quadrants of a circle, while their point of intersection symbolically represents the center of the universe. This is also the point at which the three worlds of heaven, Earth, and the midspace meet, and from which, if we take a cosmological view, the emperor is thought to be best able to sustain balance in the universe, as Chinese tradition holds he is charged with doing. Snodgrass, who adopts the same terminology as Wheatley, refers to this point as "the pivot of the four quarters." He also equates the term *pivot* with the word *gnomon,* the name that is given to the central stick of a sundial or a stupa and whose shadow indicates the hour of the day. He tells us that the oracle bone glyph *pei,* which signifies the concept of the gnomon, shows a hand holding a pole that is topped by the sun.[14]

It is within the context of this terminology that we can perhaps make sense of two Egyptian symbols that express the concept of a city or a town. These are the ⊗ glyph, which Budge identifies in his "List of Hieroglyphic Characters" as representing a "city or town," and the ▦ glyph, which visually depicts a kind of grid and which Budge defines to mean "nome or district."[15] Snodgrass and Wheatley's related symbolism of a pivot is also seemingly upheld by the written form of an Egyptian word for "palace," *apt*. This word, when read symbolically, can be interpreted to mean "that upon which space pivots."[16]

Just as geographic placements in China were meant to reflect aspects of the cosmos above, so the insistence on axiality in Chinese cities was seen as an essential link between the worlds of the microcosm and the macrocosm. This axial relationship between worlds was sustained, in part, by a topological plan that defined the descending units of nine. The Chinese emperor was the agent of this connection, and his job was to maintain harmony between the two realms. In this way, the concept of a city in China upheld a central principle of the cosmological plan as we understand it, which is expressed by the phrase "as above, so below." The meaning of this phrase is reflected in the ancient Chinese belief that placements on the ground should reflect aspects of stellar order and is reminiscent of practices that are evident in Dogon and Egyptian culture. As David W. Pankenier of Lehigh University writes in his article "Cosmic Capitals and Numinous Precincts in Early China," in reference to the astronomical alignments of an ancient Chinese temple called the Mingtang:

> Conscious imitation of the celestial patterns is perfectly consistent with the heavenward orientation of rulership in China from the outset, and in early imperial times gained physical expression, not only in the *Mingtang*, but in the imperial capital itself. There are ample historical instances of just such mimicry, which go well beyond the cardinal orientation and number symbolism of the *Mingtang*.[17]

7
DAOISM AND THE SEVEN STAGES OF CREATION

Given the many parallels we have seen so far between ancient Chinese traditions and the Dogon mythical structure of matter, it makes sense that we examine the symbolic concepts of Daoism from the perspective of this same creation theme. As one obvious point of entry to this discussion, it seems only sensible that we consider possible correlations between the Daoist concept of the seven stages of creation and the seven mythical stages of matter as they are defined in the Dogon creation tradition. (We recall that the Dogon priests count the rupturing of their egg of the world both as an eighth stage of the current "egg" and as the first stage of the next.) It has become clear from our Dogon studies and from the wealth of confirming references found in the Buddhist stupa tradition that much of the symbolic import of the number seven, as we see it exhibited again and again in the cosmologies of ancient cultures, may well have derived from this specific aspect of creation.

The conceptual stages of matter are a progression that I explored in great detail in *Sacred Symbols of the Dogon* and to which I was able to bring some new perspective through the comparison of Dogon and Egyptian cosmological words and symbols. This exercise in comparative language allowed me to recognize ongoing similarities between a number of important Dogon cosmological drawings and Egyptian glyph shapes and led me to consider the possibility that some Egyptian glyphs, along with the associated concepts they likely symbolize, may have been adapted to the needs of written language from a preexisting cosmology, which until the advent of writing had been passed down as an oral tradition.

Furthermore, we learned that, by using the Dogon creation plan as a guide and with reference to corresponding modern-day scientific concepts of matter, we could outline a sensible and scientifically reasonable progression of the formative stages of matter as it evolves from waves to the atom, given strictly in terms of Egyptian glyphs, words, and phonetic values. This process culminated in a fifteen-page table of the likely mythical stages of matter, with the heading "Structure of Matter Detail," which begins on page 114 of *Sacred Symbols of the Dogon*. Each entry in the chart refers to Egyptian words that share a common root phonetic value and that in our opinion could represent multiple meanings of the related Dogon cosmological term. Now, as we strive to understand and interpret the Daoist stages of creation, which are couched in similar mythical terminology, we begin to understand how this table might prove itself to be a worthwhile comparative tool.

As I suggested in chapter 3, while the concepts of cosmology in different cultures may sometimes be given in different languages (and therefore in terms of phonetic values that may not always match), it has been our experience that the multiple meanings associated with any given cosmological term tend to hold true without regard to the language in which they are expressed. This feature of the ancient cosmologies provides us with a reliable method to positively correlate terms. Since words in the Egyptian hieroglyphic dictionary are grouped based on spelling, not on pronunciation, these meanings tend to play out in the Egyptian hieroglyphic language as homonyms. When the spoken passages of nonliterate cultures, which were originally passed along through a mnemonic oral tradition, were eventually written down, these multidefined words often played out as wordplay or as puns. When these words were encountered by a translator who was not well versed in the underlying cosmology, unaware of the multiple definitions or without consideration of a priestly scribe whose intention it may have been to deliberately disguise from the uninitiated the true meaning of a given word, the translated meanings sometimes produced passages whose messages ring less than sensibly in the modern ear.

The word Dao itself carries the meaning of "road, path, or way" and, depending on the perspective we view it from, can convey a number of different concepts. These include an actual road for travel and the notion of a "road" that allows a person to traverse a correct spiritual path, one that proscribes the proper method of accomplishing a task, such as the alignment of a ritual structure, or that provides a correct understanding of a creation process. In our view, the word Dao correlates in one sense to an Egyptian word *uat,* meaning "way, road, path." This word is written with two glyphs. The first is a glyph, pronounced *ua,* that we associate symbolically with the concept of distance ⬚ but could also convey the notion of a journey or a road. In fact, Budge actually assigns the meaning of "way, road" to this glyph in his "List of Hieroglyphic Characters."[1] The second is the hemisphere glyph ⌒, which we associate with the concept of mass or matter in our cosmologies. Taken together and interpreted symbolically, they convey the meaning the "way, path, or road of matter"—the very subject that we believe is explicitly addressed by the seven Dogon stages of creation.[2] These are the stages of creation that also end up defining the Dogon Second World of matter, which we equate to the Egyptian underworld, and which is referred to in Egypt as the Tuat, or Duat. For both the Dogon and the Egyptians, this world is symbolized by the figure of a star (a concept defined by the Egyptian word *tua*) inscribed by a circle. The suggestion is that the term Dao in China derives from the same original cosmological concept as the terms *uat, tua,* Tuat, and Duat in Egypt.

Our understanding of the seven Daoist stages of creation comes out of a discussion by Norman J. Girardot that is set forth in his book *Myth and Meaning in Early Daoism.* Definition of these stages begins on page 119 of his book and continues through page 121. The cosmological definitions used by Girardot are drawn from chapter 2 of the *Zhuangzi*.

In the Dogon creation tradition a single set of concepts and symbols is set forth that, when considered from alternate perspectives, is said to explain concepts of both cosmological and biological creation. Although for the purposes of our discussion the emphasis on the Daoist symbolic references is cosmological in nature, the stages of creation they define are also understood in China to run parallel to comparable stages of biological creation.[3]

From the Daoist perspective, the first stage of creation is called *wuwu ruanruan*. Girardot remarks that this term is interesting in that it makes use of a rarely used character called *ruan*, which applies to the concept of wriggling, snakelike movement, or can imply a kind of embryonic life, somewhat akin to the image of a rolled-up cocoon. The Chinese term *wuwu* is a likely counterpart to the Egyptian term *uaua*, which refers to the "one and only creator of things that are."[4] The word *ua*, which in Egypt carries many different meanings that would be appropriate to our cosmology, was a title for Amen, who is the likely counterpart to the Dogon creator-god Amma. In various Egyptian dictionary word entries Budge tells us that the word *ua* can mean "one," implying the notion of "god"; it also represents the first-person singular pronoun "I," it connotes the meaning of self-creation through the meaning of "one proceeding from one," and it refers to "one who became eight," a concept that is appropriate to the eight progressive stages of matter in the Dogon tradition.

This first, not-yet-emerged stage of creation that is associated with the Chinese term *wuwu ruanruan* is described as "dipping, bending" and "flowing in waves." In keeping with a broader cosmological outlook in China that, like our other traditions, defines creation as beginning with water, we naturally associate Girardot's description with the wriggling form of the Egyptian wave glyph 〰, and the notion of wriggling and flowing in waves with the astrophysical concept of waves. Of course, the wave glyph, which carries the phonetic value *n* or *nu,* and the associated concept of matter in its wavelike form also represent a starting entry in our "Structure of Matter Detail" table in *Sacred Symbols of the Dogon.*

The Egyptian term that means "to wriggle like a serpent" is pronounced "arq."[5] It comes from a phonetic root that means "to roll up." Other word entries with the same pronunciation mean "to wrap up" or "to tie up" and "book, roll, writing," referring to a scroll. In a Jewish temple, an ark is the place where rolled Torah scrolls are kept. In the Judeo-Christian tradition, the stone tablets on which the Ten Commandments were written or inscribed are said to have been housed in the Ark of the Covenant.

Another Egyptian word entry with the same pronunciation of "arq" can also refer to "part of a chariot" and is written with the spiral glyph ℰ. This glyph shape given in the context of a chariot calls to mind a little-known astronomic structure called Barnard's Loop, which plays a central role in Dogon cosmology as a macrocosmic counterpart to the microscopic egg of the world, whose starlike rays are characterized as a spiral. Barnard's Loop was a focus of discussion in *The Cosmological Origins of Myth and Symbol.* This very faint spiraling structure, which is not readily visible to the naked eye, represents a birthplace of stars that is situated in the same direction as the constellation of Orion. The Dogon priests refer to it as the Chariot of Orion, assign great importance to the structure, and consider it to be a source of creation within our localized region of the universe. When its very faint light is imaged using time-lapse photography, the spiral of Barnard's Loop appears to coil around the belt stars of Orion and takes on the appearance of a wheel of an imagined chariot in which Orion the Hunter stands. Within this context, it seems significant that the Chinese word for "three stars," *shen,* is almost identical phonetically to the Chinese word for "chariot," which is *zhen.*

In Dogon cosmology, the second stage in the formation of matter follows an act of perception, the event that, in science, is credited with transforming matter from wavelike to particle-like behavior. The

Dogon priests say that this act of perception causes the perceived wave to be drawn upward like a tent cloth that has been pulled up from the center. They compare the resulting peak-like shape to that of an anthill. In Daoism, these processes of creation involve a vital force called *ki,* or *qi.* In the second Daoist stage of matter, ki is said to split and separate in a kind of flowing motion. This causes "Earth's ki" to descend and "heaven's ki" to rise up, a process that one might visualize in terms of two distinct but counterbalancing motions (one upward and one downward) that occur on opposing sides of a peaked tent.

The Chinese concept of the rising of ki might well correlate to an Egyptian word *khi,* which Budge defines as meaning "to raise up, to support, to be high, to rise."[6] Another Egyptian dictionary entry with the same pronunciation of "khi" remains undefined by Budge but is spelled with the three glyphs ⊜ 𓏺 𓏺, which we interpret symbolically to read "source of ⊜ existence 𓏺 𓏺." The Chinese concept of ki could also possibly relate to an Egyptian word *beqi,* which means "to flow, to descend" and whose glyphs can be read symbolically to mean "the place of earth/mass's existence."[7] The Dogon word *ki* means "to overturn, reverse, or overthrow."[8] It is the root of the Dogon cosmological term *kikinu,* which refers to a nose-shaped (in fact, tent-shaped ∧) structure that, defined within the processes of biological creation, would be comparable to a chromosome. We discussed the concept of the kikinu in greater detail in *Sacred Symbols of the Dogon.*

In the third Daoist stage of creation, heaven and Earth are said to move apart from one another to establish a kind of internal hollow that comes to be filled with the creative force of ki. This stage likely corresponds to a Dogon word *ta,* which means "to move apart, to separate." A second Dogon word entry with the same pronunciation means "to pull out, to extract from" and "to activate."[9] Supportive of this viewpoint is the Dogon word *ta:nu,* which represents the number three. In Daoism, this stage of creation is characterized by the word *glimmer.* The likely Egyptian correlate to this term is the word *tahen,* which means "to glitter, to sparkle."[10] In Egypt, the word *ta* represents the concept of

Earth and is defined by a glyph that exhibits a kind of hollow space set above three dots ⲥⲯ.[11] This glyph carries the phonetic value *ta,* and in Budge's "List of Hieroglyphic Characters" it is accompanied by two explanatory glyphs. These glyphs, when interpreted together symbolically, read "earth/mass ⌂ comes to be 𝕝."[12] Again, the hemisphere glyph presents a kind of hollow space that is defined at the top by a partial circle (the Daoist symbol for heaven) and with a base that can be seen as a partial square (the Daoist symbol for Earth).

The fourth stage of creation in Daoism involves a phase of generation that is said to precede the actual manifestation of matter and is characterized by images of roots, stems, and twigs. It likely correlates to the Egyptian deity Menu, whom Budge defines as a "god of generation."[13] Menu bears a relationship to the Egyptian word *menit,* which refers to "roots, stalks, and stems." These words are both based on a phonetic root *men,* which means "not to have" or "to be without." A symbolic reading of the glyphs with which the word *men* is written ⲙⲙⲙ ⲙⲙⲙ ⲙⲙⲙ can be interpreted to mean "waves not woven."[14] A homonym *men* means "to set down." This implies a stage of creation in which the underlying structures of matter are still being shaped or formed. We can think of them as still in the process of being manifested or as just coming into being. They have almost, but not quite, become tangible. The likely Dogon equivalent to this set of meanings is expressed by the word *manu,* which means "almost."[15] It is based on the root *ma,* which means "to mold, to shape," and likely correlates to the Egyptian *ma,* meaning "to make ready, to prepare."[16]

Girardot tells us very little about the fifth stage of creation in Daoism but implies that it defines the structures of matter in such a tentative way that, in the prior stages, matter could not have had any outward manifestation. This characterization suggests that the fifth Daoist stage of matter corresponds to the Dogon term *tonu,* which means "border or boundary." For the Dogon, matter exists in a form that constitutes a kind of outline of what eventually will become the thing to be created. The likely Egyptian correlate to this word is *teni,* which means "estimate." An Egyptian homonym for this word means "to raise, to elevate, to distinguish." The Daoist concept could also relate to an Egyptian word *tenu,* which means "piece or portion."[17]

The sixth Daoist stage of creation is described as encompassing an egg-like unity of forms in which all things were collected together into a single chaotic mass that was shaping and forging all things. This calls to mind the formation of the egg of the world in the Dogon creation tradition, the structure that results from the seven vibrations of matter. The likely Egyptian correlate is the word *sehu,* which means "to gather together, to assemble." This word forms the phonetic root of *sehu-t,* which means "egg." The Daoist suggestion of a chaotic mass is conveyed by the Egyptian word *s-hua,* meaning "to disarrange, confuse."[18] The Dogon root *se* conveys the meaning "to have, to possess, to keep." The word *senu* refers to a mass that was created by a forge.[19]

Girardot tells us that in the seventh and final stage of creation in the Daoist tradition, the cosmological process was complete and the cosmos existed in a harmonious form in which heaven and Earth (or yin and yang) were "chaotically separate," a state that Girardot defines as "chaotically fused yet distinct." He says that the Chinese term for this stage of creation means "to wrap" or "to bind," in the sense that a corpse is wrapped up. It is also linked to a word family that means "womb." In this state, Girardot says, the "world" was already present. This corresponds to a stage of matter that the Dogon priests define with the word *toymu,* meaning "complete," and which represents the culmination of the Second World of matter. On one hand, the structure is characterized by the figure of a spiral and so upholds the Daoist notion of being "wrapped up." On the other, it is characterized as seven rays of a star within a circular "egg"—essentially the symbol for the Egyptian underworld—and so is still conceptually distinct. The Dogon root *to* means "to write or to inscribe," which is a concept that the Dogon priests use to symbolize completion.[20]

The corresponding Egyptian term is *temau,* meaning "complete." The word comes from the phonetic root *tem,* which means "to make an end" and also is the name of an Egyptian deity, Tem, whom Budge defines as "the creator of heaven and earth and the womb of Tefnut." This same phoneme forms the root of the Egyptian word *tema,* which means "to bind together," and the word *tem-t,* which refers to a "bandage," which was presumably used to wrap a wound. The word *tema* refers to a "roll, book, or document." The Egyptian word *temi* or *tem-t* means "to join together," while *temm* means "to compress, to squeeze together." Like the Dogon word *to,* the Egyptian root *tem* means "to write or to inscribe."[21]

As we examine the comparative cosmological concepts of Daoism and those of the Dogon and the Egyptians, we notice a pattern relating to the Dogon and Egyptian terms that define these seven stages of matter. The majority of the concepts involve words that are based on the phonetic root *nu.* In both the Dogon and the Egyptian traditions, the term *nu* refers to the cosmological concept of the primordial waters, which is deemed to be a starting point for cosmological creation. The suggestion is that, within the common system of cosmology that appears to be reflected in these cultures, the seven stages of matter may have been originally defined by a set of phonetically related terms. From this perspective, the stages could be given as follows:

1	*Nu/Nua/Ua*	The primordial waters (matter as waves)
2	*Benu*	Self-produced
3	*Tanu/Ta*	Move apart
4	*Menu*	Preparation
5	*Tonu/Teni*	Boundary, border, estimate
6	*Senu*	Egg, gather together, assemble
7	*Temau*	Complete (Calabi-Yau space)

Based on prior Dogon and Egyptian studies, we can add to this list at least two more defined stages of matter. These would be:

8	*Aunnu*	To vibrate or open (electron)
9	*Pau/Po*	Existence (mass/matter/atom)

We notice in this list of terms that the phonetic value changes from "nu" to "au" at the two points of conceptual completion. The finished egg of the world associates with the term *temau,* and mass or matter in its completed state associates with the term *pau.* All other intermediate stages are expressed in terms of the *nu* suffix.

Symbolism in the Dogon tradition is given in terms of a series of sets of four-stage metaphors that help guide an initiate through the complex system of symbols and symbolic concepts. These define four distinct categories of symbols, which by way of the various metaphors are offered from differing perspectives. The first of these is given from the perspective of a person who builds a structure but is applicable to any considered endeavor. It is expressed in terms that closely resemble the seven stages discussed in this chapter and can be characterized as defining the generic pattern for the other metaphors. They are defined by the terms *bummo, yala, tonu,* and *toymu.* The term *bummo* combines the first two Daoist categories and represents a conceptual stage in which the project exists only as an idea. The comparable Egyptian term is *bu maa,* which we interpret symbolically to mean "place perceived." The second term, *yala,* corresponds to the third and fourth stages in Daoism and represents a stage in which the project exists in outline form. The comparable Egyptian term is *ahau,* which refers to "delimitation posts." By the third stage, *tonu,* the boundaries of the project have been defined. This corresponds to the Egyptian word *teni,* meaning "estimate." The project comes to completion in a fourth stage, *toymu,* which corresponds to the seventh stage of creation in Daoism. In Egyptian the term is *temau,* which means "complete."

As we suggested, this first set of defined categories establishes a pattern for similar groupings of metaphoric categories. These metaphors play out in similar form to the four primordial elements of water, fire, wind, and earth. One of the metaphors is given in terms of the stages of growth of a plant from a seed; another is given in terms of the growth of a bird from an egg. Two others are expressed in terms of the formation of a spoken word from an initial sound and a written word from a drawn sign. Still another is defined in terms of four classes of living creatures and is given as insects, fish, four-legged animals, and birds. These well-defined progressions provide us with important reference points by which to understand the relative stage of creation that is represented by a given symbol we may encounter within the cosmology.

There is also the clear suggestion of a relationship between the seven Daoist stages of creation and the simple act of counting with numbers. Girardot characterized the Daoist descriptions of creation in the *Zhuangzi* as being "numerically coded" and expressed as an exercise in counting, wherein:

> *"The Dao gave birth to the one.*
> *The one gave birth to the two.*
> *The two gave birth to the three . . ."*

And so on.[22] The Egyptian words that we correlate to these stages convey the impression of a similar exercise in counting. On page 80, we mentioned that the Egyptian word *ua,* which corresponds to the first stage of creation, refers to the concept of the one, or the creator. In our discussions of the third stage of Daoist creation we mentioned possible relationships to the number three and the Egyptian glyph pronounced "ta." The fifth Daoist stage of creation, which we correlate to the Dogon word *tonu,* bears a phonetic resemblance to the Egyptian word for "five," which is pronounced "tu." So, although the correspondence is not altogether precise, it seems possible (if not likely) that these progressive stages of creation were tagged to the notion of counting in the original plan of our cosmology.

Dogon cosmology defines an eighth stage of matter that can actually be seen simply as an eventual consequence of the seventh Daoist stage. As we have mentioned, the Dogon priests conceptualize these processes of the creation of matter as seven rays of a star of increasing length that evolve within the confines of a kind of egg. They characterize this structure in terms of the spiral that can be drawn to inscribe the endpoints of these rays. The Dogon say that the seventh ray grows long enough to actually pierce the egg, an eventuality that simultaneously marks the end of the first egg and initiates the formation of a second egg. Unlike the seven Daoist stages of creation, this act of piercing is counted in the Dogon tradition as a discrete eighth stage.

8

THE MANDALA

The mandala is widely recognized as a central symbol of Chinese cosmology, in much the same way that the figure is treated as sacred in the cosmologies of India and other parts of Asia. In *The Symbolism of the Stupa,* Adrian Snodgrass tells us that, although it can take many diverse forms, the mandala is basically a circle that has been inscribed inside a square, once again bringing its meaning around to the symbolic squaring of a circle. He tells us that the geometric characteristics of a mandala are effectively the same as the characteristics of the plan of a Buddhist stupa. Further affirmation for the parallels we have described in our studies between the Buddhist and Dogon ritual shrines is found in Carl Jung's book *Mandala Symbolism.* Here Jung provides us with a positive link between the circular plan of the mandala and the egg-in-a-ball figure as it is described by the Dogon priests when he states that, in the study of alchemy, the circle of the mandala represents the synthesis of the four primordial elements.[1]

Snodgrass overtly tells us that, like a stupa, the mandala is laid out in accordance with ritualized principles that define the "squaring of the circle."[2] This view is again echoed by Jung, who also explicitly associates the principles of the squaring a circle with the mandala and considers this concept to be "one of the many archetypical motifs" that form the basis of human psychology and dreams.[3] If we look at the mandala in terms of known Chinese symbolism of geometric shapes as discussed in previous chapters, wherein a circle is taken to represent the concept of heaven and the square to represent the concept of Earth, then the mandala can be seen as a figure that reconciles the relationship between the two concepts. To the extent that a mandala is like the plan of a stupa, we can say that its form also illustrates the fundamental principles of the ordering of space.

In keeping with these parallels between the mandala and the base plan of a stupa, it is interesting that initiates to the Tibetan Buddhist tantric tradition are routinely taught to design mandalas and are ultimately expected to be able to do so from memory. We can see from figure 8.1 that the method used to plot these figures is outwardly similar to the geometry that is used to align a Buddhist stupa. Early in their initiation process Buddhist initiates construct temporary mandalas out of colored sand, which are typically displayed on a raised terrace or platform. The central square of the mandala is measured as 8 × 8 proportional units, the same as the measure in cubits of the square roof of a Dogon granary. These are the same dimensions that also represent the traditional measurements of a Vedic altar.[4]

Both Jung and Snodgrass report that, in Sanskrit, the word *mandala* means "circle." Snodgrass tells us that it also implies the concept of a "centered space," a space that has been enclosed and made sacred so

Figure 8.1. Geometric plan of a mandala

as to facilitate ritual acts. In Buddhism, the term for a mandala is *dkyil khor,* which means "center circumference," a definition that describes the basic geometry of a mandala.[5] This definition also calls to mind the circular sun glyph shape ⊙, the same configuration that constitutes the base plan of a stupa and that serves as the foundation for the Dogon egg-in-a-ball figure. One commentary states that the center of the mandala represents the *essence,* and that its circumference represents the *grasping of that essence.*[6] For the Dogon priests, the egg-in-a-ball figure is alternately defined as a picture of Amma, the creator-god who represents the source or essence of creation and whose name also means "to grasp."

In Chinese texts, the Sanskrit word for mandala is at times simply transliterated as *man t'u lo* or can be translated to the Chinese term *t'an,* meaning "terrace, platform, world, or arena." We can see that this translated meaning reflects a definition of the location in which a Buddhist initiate is traditionally taught to construct a mandala. In Tibet, the term for mandala means "center" or "what surrounds."[7] The diagram Snodgrass provides to illustrate his concept of a mandala is that of a circle inscribed in a square, aligned to a three-dimensional axis that passes through its center. The square is subdivided into a grid that measures eight units per side. We can positively relate the concept of the mandala to the philosophies of Daoism through a Chinese term given to it, *tao tch'ang,* which means "place of the way."

Snodgrass goes on to say that the meaning of *circle* as it relates to the word *mandala* also applies to a group of people, conceptualized in the familiar modern sense as "a circle of friends." In this context, the term implies the concept of completeness, a symbolic notion that is conveyed by the image of a "closed circle."

Without regard to Snodgrass's statement that explicitly equates the plan of a mandala to the base plan of a Buddhist stupa (and by inference a Dogon granary), we can relate the figure of the mandala to the seven vibrations of the Dogon egg in a ball through the term that is given to the staged process by which a mandala is laid out on the ground, which is called the seven-day ritual. We can again correlate the mandala to the egg in a ball by way of the overt cosmological symbolism that is traditionally assigned to it. Just as the egg in a ball symbolically evokes pairs of Dogon ancestors whose growth is alternately compared to seeds, in Japan the mandala is said to give birth to Buddhas in the metaphoric sense that it gives growth to the "seed of Buddhism." This is a seed that is seen to sprout after years of careful study on the part of Buddhist initiates.[8] From this perspective, a Buddha can be said to align conceptually with the Dogon concept of an ancestor. It is from cosmological references similar to these seed-related ones, which are given by the Dogon priests in the context of a discussion of the growth of matter, that the symbolism of growth comes to be assigned to the Egyptian sprout glyph 𓇇.

Although the mandala is not a form that is outwardly associated with ancient Egypt, we can see that many of the terms that Snodgrass uses to define the word *mandala* also exist in similar form in the Egyptian hieroglyphic dictionary, associated with words that stem from the phonetic root *ma*. Budge defines one Egyptian word *ma* as meaning "to wrap up in," a meaning that reflects Snodgrass's sense of "to surround."[9] Another word entry for *ma* is defined as "a gathering of people," which again expresses Snodgrass's notion of a "circle of friends." A third Egyptian word entry means "altar, slab, table for offering," and so conveys the image of a sacred "terrace or platform." The concurrence of these meanings in the Egyptian hieroglyphic language suggests that the concept of a mandala in these other cultures was given in accordance with the multiple meanings that typify terms within our cosmology.

Snodgrass tells us that in China, the word *mandala* combines the word *manda*, which refers to a concentrated essence of milk called *ghee*, and the word *la*, which means "composed of." Taken together, the symbolism of these terms implies that the mandala represents a kind of distilled essence of the universe.[10]

Budge defines no Egyptian word comparable to the "distilled essence of milk." However, it is interesting that the Egyptian word *gi*, a likely phonetic counterpart to the Chinese *ghee,* actually refers to a "terrace." Symbolically this word reads "terrace ⬚ of ⎮ ⎮ steps ◿," which is a fairly apt description of a Dogon granary or stupa. This word provides both the phonetic and written-glyph root of the word *gi-t,* which Budge defines as "a plant or herb." Symbolically, the word *gi-t* reads "terrace ⬚ of ⎮ ⎮ mass ◠," followed by the three-pronged plant glyph that we have associated in previous volumes with the tree of life. I argued that this glyph represents a symbol for the stages of the growth of matter, a process that is conceptualized by the Dogon as traversing three worlds.[11]

Mark Edward Lewis states that the most prominent architectural form associated with the ancient Chinese city, whose plan seems to relate to the mandala form, was a raised terrace or platform called *tai.*[12] This term calls to mind ancient Egyptian words formed on the phonetic value *ta,* which include concepts that relate to divine emanation—the process by which matter is said to be evoked. This phonetic value is also associated with two Egyptian glyphs that are included in Budge's "List of Hieroglyphic Characters." The first glyph, in our view, symbolizes the process of divine emanation ◿. The second glyph we interpret as an alternate to the hemisphere glyph, which in our view relates to the concept of mass, matter, or earth ⬱. Both are given by Budge in conjunction with the same two explanatory glyphs: ◠ 🦅. Symbolically, we interpret these explanatory glyphs to read "earth/mass ◠ comes to be 🦅."

In accordance with the dual symbolism of Dogon cosmology, in which the symbolic ritual structure of the granary is equated with the concept of a womb, Snodgrass tells us that the Chinese and Japanese glyph *tai* is used interchangeably to express the concept of a storehouse and the concept of a womb. When considered from the perspective of biological reproduction, the cosmological concept of "mass coming to be" can be seen to run parallel to the notion of the growth of a womb during the weeks of a pregnancy, as it increases in both size and mass.

Snodgrass explains that the plan of a mandala is laid out on the ground and is meant to define the area it comprises as sacred space, thereby making that space ready and suitable for the performance of ritual acts. This same idea seems to be conveyed by the Egyptian word *ma*, which means "to make ready, to prepare." Finally, and perhaps most significantly, the idea that the plan of a mandala represents a fundamental ordering of space appears to be conveyed by the Egyptian term *m'aat*, which means "order."[13] This concept of m'aat is traditionally considered to be one of the conceptual foundations of ancient Egyptian culture. It represents the overriding cosmological principle that the pharaoh was said to embody and that he was expressly charged with upholding and preserving in Egyptian society.

In *Architecture, Time, and Eternity*, Adrian Snodgrass argues that the plan of the ancient Chinese city also represented a ninefold mandala, a figure that corresponds to the image of nine squares of land discussed in chapter 5. In Snodgrass's view, this configuration of space lay at the heart of the concept of Chinese land division. We may recall that this organizational concept was applied at all levels of Chinese geography, beginning with the continents and culminating in the well-field system that was used to define agricultural plots.[14] Snodgrass's viewpoint echoes that of Paul Wheatley, who also clearly stated his own personal conviction that the plan of the Chinese city was based on the concept of the mandala.[15]

9

THE YIJING (I CHING)

Richard Smith, in his work *Fathoming the Cosmos and Ordering the World: The Yijing (I-Ching, or Classic of Changes) and Its Evolution in China,* describes the *Yijing,* or *Book of Changes,* as "the most important single book in China's entire philosophical tradition."[1] Smith tells us that many of the philosophical concepts on which the book is based are overtly cosmological in nature, so it is not surprising that Confucius characterized the book as containing "the Dao of Heaven, the Dao of Man, and the Dao of Earth." In fact, it is Smith's belief, based on references in the great commentary on the *Book of Changes* known as the *Dazhuan,* that the book can be seen as an effective microcosm of the fundamental processes of the universe.[2] Although on one level the *Book of Changes* has been purported to be easy to understand, it touches on fundamental philosophies that, when more carefully considered, can become quite complex. Over the centuries the book has spawned literally thousands of different commentaries. These have been given from the perspectives of a wide range of disciplines, to each of which the teachings of the *Yijing* are said to directly pertain. Consequently, the *Yijing* has become perhaps the most influential and controversial book in the history of China.

Like other important aspects of Chinese cosmology, the precise origins of the *Yijing* are not known with certainty. Concepts expressed in the book are thought to have predated the advent of writing in China, so they would be contemporaneous with the ancient cosmologies discussed in our studies. Some scholars consider the *Book of Changes* to be merely a random collection of ideas that emerged over time and were related to the act of divination. Other researchers see signs in the book of careful, deliberate design. The trail of evidence pertinent to the origin of the book is again complicated by the fact that the earliest written records that document its history date from many centuries (and perhaps millennia) after the ideas expressed in the book are thought to have first been developed.[3]

Because many of the concepts presented in the *Book of Changes* seem to be cosmological in nature, may be contemporaneous with our plan of cosmology, and appear to share common roots with Daoist concepts we have already discussed, it seems reasonable to think that we might find correlates to its teachings in the Dogon and Egyptian cosmological traditions. The first and most obvious of these correlates derives from the Chinese name for the book itself. Smith tells us that the Chinese term *yi* (pronounced "i"), which means "change," should actually be translated in the singular, since its meaning is defined as the concept of *change in the state of something,* rather than actual *changes through which a person or thing might pass.*

When we look to the Dogon dictionary for parallel concepts, we find that the word entry *i* refers to "a suffix that also indicates state or condition."[4] Likewise, in ancient Egypt, Budge tells us that a word he tenuously believes to have been pronounced "aiu" means "change or transformation." This word is based on the phonetic root *ai,* which means "to be," the same verb by which concepts that relate to "state of condition" are expressed. Budge's Egyptian word entry that means "to be" is written with two spellings that are explicitly equated with one another. By our symbolic interpretation, the first reads "that which ⟨ exists ⟨ ⟨," and the second "that which ⟨ grows/changes ⟐." The word that represents the concept of change repeats the very same characters found in these two spellings of "to be" and so reads "that which exists and grows/changes ," but it is followed by the image of a scroll. In the conventions of the Egyptian hieroglyphic language, a scroll determinative is typically used to convey the notion of something that has been physically written.[5] This implies that this Egyptian term for "change" may actually refer to a text or a book of change similar to what we find in China.

Chinese tradition holds that the foundations of the *Yijing* were set down by the Sage King Fu-Xi when he invented eight three-lined symbols called trigrams (or *gua*) to represent the innate forms of the universe (figure 9.1).

Smith believes that the concepts of the *Yijing* originally bore a relationship to the cardinal numbers, which in Egypt were written with a series of strokes or lines: | || ||| ||||. Likewise, Budge, in his "List of Hieroglyphic Characters," assigns the phonetic value "i" to two vertical strokes | |, which are alternately given as two reed leaf glyphs, the same glyphs that we interpret to represent the concept of existence and that form the basis of the Egyptian words that mean "to be" and "change." From this perspective, we see a possible relationship between the Dogon, Egyptian, and Chinese concepts for "change" expressed with both matched phonetic values and matched symbols.[6]

Figure 9.1. The eight trigrams

The Chinese term *gua* is a likely correlate to the Egyptian word *kha,* which refers to the concept of manifestation. This phonetic value is the root of the Egyptian word *khap,* which means "form, image, similitude." In the Dogon tradition, the familiar structures of matter we perceive are described by the Dogon priests as constituting a mere image or reflection of a more fundamental underlying reality.[7]

This Egyptian word *khap* is written with the ⊜ glyph—a circle that, like the trigrams of the *Yijing,* encloses a series of strokes or lines.[8] It is a glyph that, within the context of our discussions of Dogon and Egyptian cosmology, we have said represents the concepts of source and product or result and can be used to symbolize the primordial source of matter. Budge assigns a phonetic pronunciation of "kh" to this glyph, a value that, as the root of the word *khi,* we believe bears a likely relationship to the Chinese concept of qi. The Egyptian word *khi* refers to the energy or life force that arises from the primordial source. In the shorthand of our cosmologies, the primordial source is a notion that we identify with the mythical element of water and the scientific concept of matter in its wavelike form. From this perspective, the glyph could represent a pool of water, the same image that, in Chinese cosmology, is said to rest at the base of the mulberry tree.

Budge also refers to an Egyptian god named Kha, whose role he does not actually define. However, we can see based on a conceptual reading of the symbols used to write Kha's name that he likely represents a cosmological effect that we associate with the manifestation of particles—the concept of an increase in mass. The name Kha is written symbolically as "increased mass 𐦀," followed by the *neter* flag ⌐ (the use of a *neter* flag implies a relationship to the mother goddess Neith, or Net, who is credited with having woven matter) and the god determinative 𓀀.[9] Mass is a concept that we associate with the primordial element earth, based on definitions given commonly in the Dogon and Buddhist traditions. The term *manifestation* represents a concept that we assigned to the primordial element fire. In support of both the meaning of the Chinese term *gua* as representing forms that arise and are differentiated from the primordial source and its likely correlation to the Egyptian root *kha,* we note that Genevieve Calame-Griaule defines the Dogon word *kaba* as meaning "to separate or distinguish."[10] Taken together, these references lend support to the notion that the Chinese gua, or trigrams, do in fact bear a likely symbolic relationship to primordial structures that are manifested during the formation of matter.

In each of the ancient cosmological traditions we have studied, one primary consequence of the processes of creation is that they serve to separate earth from sky. Earth and sky are symbolic terms that, on one level, we believe correlate in science to the notion of mass as it is differentiated from space. In the Dogon creation tradition, this differentiation is said to come about when threads of matter pass through a series of vibrations that are characterized as a spiral. Within the ancient plan of cosmology, the concept of vibration is symbolized by the term *wind,* a concept that we associate—based on a symbolic reading of an Egyptian defining word and the glyph's resemblance to a Dogon field drawing—with the Egyptian town glyph ⊗.[11]

In some ancient traditions, this separation between earth and sky is said to be sustained by four pillars or columns. In the Egyptian hieroglyphic language, the term *kha* also refers to the notion of a column. From the perspective of our symbolic approach to reading Egyptian hieroglyphic words, this word constitutes a defining word for the wind glyph ⊤, a figure that for us symbolizes the concept of vibration. Symbolically the word *kha* reads "the primordial source ⊜ comes to be 🐦 a spiral ℂ," followed by the wind glyph ⊤. A second spelling for the same word qualifies as a defining word for both the vibration/town glyph ⊗ and for the branch glyph ⤞. Using terminology we established in *Sacred Symbols of the Dogon,* an Egyptian word whose meaning defines more than one related glyph is called an enumerating definition.[12] Symbolically, this second spelling reads "increased mass ⌇ comes to grow 🐦," followed by the branch glyph ⤞ and the vibration/town glyph ⊗. Budge also gives a second spelling for the deity Kha that qualifies as a defining word for the vibration/town glyph ⊗.

These references, taken together, would seem to tie the notion of kha to the primordial element of wind.

We can see from the preceding discussion that the Egyptian concept of kha seems to bear a symbolic relationship to concepts that pertain to the source of primordial creation. However, our proposed symbolic definitions for these words leave us in the somewhat uncomfortable position of having associated all four of the primordial elements of water, fire, wind, and earth with the concepts of khi and kha. This development seemingly contradicts the rules of symbolism as we understand them to typically work within our system of cosmology. Until now, our expectation has been that each cosmological term will associate with only a single symbolic concept; otherwise, a great deal of confusion might result when trying to establish a discrete meaning to be applied to a given symbol. So in regard to the term *kha,* the immediate question arises of how and why a single phonetic value could reasonably come to be associated with all four primordial elements.

However, if we rely again on linguistic parallels that, for important cosmological terms, appear to cross cultural boundaries, a reasonable answer to this question soon becomes apparent. Richard Smith tells us that the transformations associated with the seven stages of Daoist creation are defined by the term *bian.* This Chinese word implies the notion of "changes in state or alternations occurring in turn."[13] We see the word *bian* as a likely correlate to the Dogon word *bia,* which means "change of form." Genevieve Calame-Griaule clarifies the specific sense of meaning conveyed by the Dogon word by comparing it to the process by which gelatin gels.[14] (In a similar context, Marcel Griaule also compares the transformations of matter to changes in the state of water, which can take the form of a liquid, solid ice, or water vapor.) This same word, *bia,* provides the likely phonetic and conceptual root for the name of a traditional ritual Dogon shrine called the *binu.* The binu is a totemic shrine on whose outer walls a series of cosmological images are traditionally painted—images that also play a role in Dogon cosmological descriptions of the transformation of matter.

The Yijing (I Ching)   101

In light of the relationships that are thought to exist between the trigrams of the *Yijing* and both the cardinal numbers and the mythical Fu-xi who ostensibly conceived them, it is interesting to note that the Egyptian word *fu* represents the number four. By our symbolic interpretation, this word reads "that by which ⟨ transmission ⟳ is given ⟱."[15] A second Egyptian word for "four" is given by Budge as *ftu.* Symbolically it reads "transmission ⟳ is given ⟱ to mass/matter △."[16] Budge defines a third Egyptian word for "four" that is pronounced "aft." Symbolically it reads "that by which ⟨ transmission ⟳ is given ⟱ to mass/matter △."[17] But what is perhaps more interesting is the fact that this word is based on the phonetic root *af,* which means "to turn, to twist, to revolve."[18] The concept of waves turning and twisting in the shape of a spiral is one that plays an important role in Dogon descriptions of the formation of matter. The discovery of this concept in relation to the Egyptian number four suggests that it could play a similar role in ancient Chinese concepts of creation.

Smith tells us that the second portion of the word Yijing is based on the word *ji,* which characterizes these initial stirrings of matter, and he suggests that the type of movement implied should be compared to that of a door hinge, a trigger, or a pivot. Again, the use of the term *pivot* immediately calls to mind Paul Wheatley's discussions of the base plan of the Chinese city that centers on an axis, a central theme of ancient Chinese cosmology that Wheatley refers to as "the pivot of the four quarters" and that defines a conceptual starting point for the processes of creation. We have said that this civic plan mirrors the layout of the Dogon egg-in-a-ball figure, where a circle that is divided into four quarters by two axes is said to symbolize the four primordial elements of water, wind, earth, and fire. Considered from this perspective, we see that the number four in the Chinese tradition can, in fact, reasonably be said to relate to all four primordial elements, just as the symbolism of the Egyptian word *kha* seems to imply they should.

Furthermore, as Wheatley writes (and we have mentioned in chapter 6), there is an alternate interpretation of the Chinese civic plan wherein the central point at which the two axes meet is replaced conceptually by four squares. These are most typically conceived of as four squares arranged to make yet another larger square. However, Adrian Snodgrass tells us that the reference is ambiguous as to the configuration, and so some Chinese scholars believe that these squares should properly align to one another in the shape of a cross, not as a square. This alternate alignment provides us with a functional description of (and a sensible explanation for the form and symbolism of) the Egyptian town glyph ⊗. Furthermore, the arrangement of four squares in the shape of a cross can actually be seen to define nine-squared spaces, a configuration that represents the traditional layout of land plots in the well-field system.

In overt support of these observations based on the symbolism of the Chinese term *ji*, we also offer the Dogon word *jige*, which means "to oscillate or vibrate." Genevieve Calame-Griaule tells us that the concept of jige refers to an initial vibration and turning of space that culminates in the formation of matter. In the *Dictionnaire Dogon*, she explains that this initial vibration of the primordial waters induces the threads of matter (symbolized by the four primordial elements) to begin to turn in the shape of a spiral. The flat plane in which these elements originally exist is transformed by these vibrations into the shape of a chevron, a form that is (as discussed in chapter 7) essentially the shape of a raised tent ∧. To illustrate the proper motion associated with this concept of turning, she includes an illustration as part of her dictionary definition. The figure is essentially that of a thin crossbar that has a weighted ball attached to each of its two ends. This crossbar balances and pivots on an elevated point. She states that this sense of transformation and pivoting lies at the very heart of the Dogon concept of creation. Our contention is that Calame-Griaule's description is of the very same pivoting motion that is referred to by Paul Wheatley and that also characterizes the Chinese definition of the term *ji*. In this way, both terms can be seen to effectively illustrate Wheatley's concept of the pivot of the four quarters.[19]

10
THE EIGHT TRIGRAMS

Although our discussion of the implications of the term Yijing seems to play out in a fairly straightforward way, the question of what the original intent may have been behind the symbolism of the eight trigram figures may prove to be somewhat less overt. We have mentioned that the Chinese term for the eight trigrams is *gua*. In fact, the full term is given alternately as *ba gua* or *pa gua*.[1] Again we gain likely insight into the meanings of the words in these terms when we look to definitions from our comparative cultures. The entry in the *Dictionnaire Dogon* for *ba* tells us that the word likely refers to the concept of vibration, this time given in relation to the notion of the beating of a drum.[2] Likewise, we find that the Dogon word *gua* means "concealed." Taken together, the Dogon words convey the meaning of "concealed vibrations." Similarly, we know that the Egyptian word *pa* refers to the concept of existence and bears an apparent relationship to the concept of the po, which is the mythical Dogon counterpart to an atom.[3] From this perspective, the term *pa gua* would imply the concept of "concealed existence." Either definition would be appropriate to the initial stirrings of wave-like matter in a scientific description of the processes of creation. Confirmation for this view is found in the form of the Egyptian word *tekhen,* which means "to beat a drum." The symbolic form of this word, ⌒ ⊜ 𓀾 ⌐, implies the sense of the meaning "the act by which matter is manifested from the source." A second Egyptian word, *tekhen,* means "to hide."[4] We know, as per our discussion in chapter 9, that in the traditional view of Chinese scholars, there are likely associations between the eight trigrams and the cardinal numbers from one to eight. Smith also defines symbolic terms that correlate each of the eight trigrams to a primordial element. These two concurrent levels of symbolism are reminiscent of the dual, logically distinct definitions that are characteristic of important words as they are given within our plan of cosmology. In the past, we have found these variant definitions to be invaluable to our attempts to correlate cosmological concepts between cultures.

Furthermore, it seems apparent from our examination of concepts that relate to the *Yijing* that we can expect to find a high degree of commonality between the Chinese, Dogon, and Egyptian terms used to define the symbolism of the trigrams, as well as between the phonetic values in which those terms and symbolic definitions are expressed. So it seems completely sensible that we continue our exploration of the

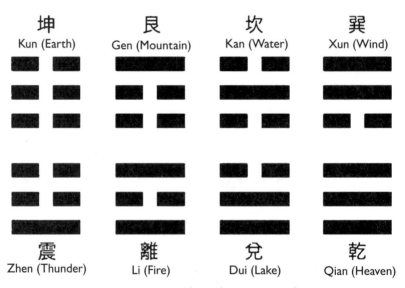

*Figure 10.1. The eight trigrams of
the I Ching, or Yijing*

concept of the trigrams using the same methods we have employed up to this point, first and foremost by pursuing various linguistic clues that may exist between the languages of the cultures involved.

The original eight trigrams of the *Yijing* are typically given as sets of strokes that are grouped to form eight square figures (figure 10.1). For these discussions, the trigrams are read from bottom to top, moving from right to left.

In accordance with the likely number symbolism that is thought to have been originally associated with these figures, our best approach for discussion may be to address their symbolic attributes one at a time. It also makes sense to present this discussion in what, by our interpretation, would be the proper numerical order. It is important to bear in mind during this discussion that an Egyptian number can be associated with more than one word and that any cosmological term given in the language of one culture may well not have survived in the language of another.

THE FIRST TRIGRAM

The Chinese term *qian,* which Richard Smith associates with the concept of heaven, likely relates to the Egyptian word *khi*. Entries for this word in the Egyptian hieroglyphic dictionary appear to satisfy both symbolic requirements of the trigram, which imply a relationship both to a cardinal number and to the primordial element heaven or sky. Budge tells us that the word *khi* refers to both the concept of heaven and the notion of the exalted one, God.[5] By our standards, symbolically the word for heaven constitutes a defining word for the sky glyph ⌐⌐ and reads "source ⊜ of \\ existence ⎨ ⎨," followed by the sky glyph ⌐⌐.

THE SECOND TRIGRAM

Moving to a second trigram, we see that the term *xun* (Smith actually transliterates the word as *sun*) is assigned to this figure. This trigram is associated with the primordial element wind, which, cosmologically, we take to symbolize the concept of vibration. We view this Chinese term as a likely correlate to the Egyptian word *sen*. Both the masculine and feminine forms of the word (*senui* and *senti,* respectively) mean "two," while the word *sen* itself implies the concept of being "dual."[6] We recall from our discussion in chapter 9 that the Egyptian town glyph ⊗ is associated with the concept of the vibrations of matter. The Dogon field drawing that correlates to this figure is actually said to symbolize all of the possible vibrations of matter. However, in previous volumes of this series we have also identified Egyptian references to vibration that are expressed symbolically through other glyphs, including the wave glyph. This glyph takes the same up/down graphic form as a typical scientific graph that is used to illustrate the frequency of a given vibration. Taken in this context, a symbolic interpretation of the word *sen* reads "the other � vibration 〰."[7]

THE THIRD TRIGRAM

The Chinese trigram *dui,* which Smith relates to the concept of a lake, is a likely correlate to an Egyptian word entry pronounced "tui," whose meaning Budge does not actually define. Symbolically the word reads "mass/matter ⌒ grows 🐦, existence ⎪ ⎪ is spoken 🐒," and is followed by three stroke-lines ⦙, which by Egyptian notational conventions could in this case imply the number three. This word provides a phonetic root for the word *tun,* which means "rising flood, inundation," a meaning that could correspond to the Chinese term for a lake. Symbolically, the word *tun* includes the rabbit or hare glyph 🐇, an animal that, from the standpoint of our cosmologies, yet again represents the concept of vibration, this time symbolized by the animal's tendency to twitch. The word reads "matter ⌒ vibrates 🐇," followed by three clay pot glyphs ○ ○ ○, which once again could imply the number three, and the sky glyph ▭.[8]

THE FOURTH TRIGRAM

The Egyptian number four is a concept we have already discussed in chapter 9 in relation to the Egyptian word *fu,* which means "four." Although the Egyptian word bears no phonetic resemblance to the Chinese term *kan,* we recall that the term *four* implies the concept of the four quarters. This refers to a configuration similar to the Dogon egg-in-a-ball figure that is given to represent the concept of the four elements, all in relation to a symbolic representation of how creation emerges from the primordial waters.

THE FIFTH TRIGRAM

The concept of the number five is given by the Egyptian word *tu,* which is unrelated phonetically to the Chinese term for the number, *li.* The word *tu* is represented alternately by five stroke-lines or by a five-rayed star. In Dogon cosmology, the initial vibrations of matter are conceptualized as rays of a star. The Egyptian word for "fifth" is *tu-nu* and is given as five stroke-lines followed by the clay pot glyph ○ and the hemisphere glyph ◠, which we recognize as symbols for the concepts of a particle and of mass or matter. Another Egyptian dictionary entry for the word *tu* means "hill, mountain." It is written with the hill or mountain glyph ᴍᴍ (a shape that exhibits a total of five peaks and valleys) and can be followed by the hemisphere glyph ◠.

THE SIXTH TRIGRAM

The Egyptian number six is represented by the word *sas,* which bears no apparent phonetic relationship to the Chinese numerical term for six, *gen.* The word *sas* is written with six stroke-lines, followed by the clay pot glyph ○ and the hemisphere glyph ◠, which again refer symbolically to a "particle of mass/matter."[9] The word *sas* is based on the phonetic root *sa*, which means "fire or flame." Symbolically it reads "the binding —∘— of the spoken word 𓀁 that is the spiral ℃," followed by the fire glyph 𓏲.[10]

THE SEVENTH TRIGRAM

By our interpretation, the trigram *zhen* represents the number seven. In Egypt, this number is given with the word *sefekh*. Budge presents one spelling of this word that includes seven stroke-lines followed by the hemisphere glyph △, which we read to mean "the seventh stage |||| ||| of mass/matter △."[11] This trigram corresponds to the concept of thunder, a natural event that is characterized by a loud sound. Consequently, Egyptian words for thunder are often homonyms for words that pertain to the act of a person who speaks in a loud voice. This imagery is consistent with Dogon cosmology, where on one level the last of the vibrations of matter are compared to the speaking of the Word. From this perspective, we see a likely relationship to the Egyptian word *shen,* which means "to proclaim," a phoneme that forms the root of words that mean "tempest," a weather event that is characterized by thunder. Symbolically, the word *shen* reads "the binding of ◌ vibration ∿ is \\ spoken 𓀁."[12]

THE EIGHTH TRIGRAM

On yet another level of Dogon cosmological symbolism that relates to stages in the weaving of a cloth, the eighth and final stage of vibration is the point at which matter said to be "woven." This represents the final creative stage of the egg of the world, which is defined as the smallest discrete particle-like structure of matter. The Egyptian word for "eight" is *khemen* and reads symbolically "product of ⊜ woven ▭▭ vibrations ∿." In an alternate spelling it is also given as two sets of four stroke-lines that flank the symbol of a clay pot ○, which in our cosmology symbolizes the concept of a particle, and as a spiral ℃, the shape that characterizes the eighth stage of matter in Dogon cosmology. Budge interprets the Egyptian word *khemen-t* to refer to "a kind of stuff, eight-thread cloth." By our standard of symbolic interpretation, this word defines the hemisphere glyph ⌒, which we take as a symbol for mass or matter and as a counterpart to the cosmological concept of earth.[13]

As an incidental note, the word *khem* is an ancient term for the land of Egypt itself. Other entries for the word in Budge's dictionary call to mind symbolism that we associate with the name of the Dogon tribe. Griaule and Dieterlen tell us that the word Dogon, like other Dogon cosmological terms, carries twin meanings—in this case, "to complete the words" and "to remain silent" or "to feign ignorance." We understand these definitions to represent the two primary obligations of a priest in the Dogon esoteric tradition. When an initiate asks an appropriate question about the cosmology, a priest is required to answer truthfully so as to help bring the initiate's education to the point of completion. When any person asks a question about the cosmology that is inappropriate to his or her initiated status, the priest is obliged to remain silent or to lie if necessary to protect privileged cosmological knowledge. Budge tells us that the Egyptian word *khem* means "to bring an end to." The same word also means "to feign ignorance."[14] The concurrence of these meanings in the Dogon and Egyptian words constitutes a second likely naming convention for the ancient tribes who preserved our plan of cosmology.

The Egyptian word *khem*—taken in light of the two predominant Egyptian theologies that centered on the eight paired Ennead and Ogdoad gods and goddesses—suggests that one of the original tribal names for ancient Egypt may have implied that Egypt "celebrated eight" in much the same way that the name Fu-xi suggests that an ancient Chinese tribe "celebrated four."

It is interesting to note that the eight trigrams of the *Yijing* as set out in the figure that begins this chapter are already presented in what we deem to be the correct numerical sequence, given their likely correlation to Egyptian words and numbers. But this is true only if we read the figures from right to left, and as if in columns, starting at the bottom and moving to the top. This unexpected arrangement calls to mind the various arrangements that can properly apply to the writing of an Egyptian hieroglyphic word or text and to the Hebrew language, whose characters are read from right to left. It also recalls a similar arrangement of images in the Dogon figure that is given to represent the stages of vibration of matter (figure 10.2). These vibrations occur within the Dogon *po pilu*, or egg of the world, and the component figures used to represent these vibrations are also read from right to left. These figures begin (at the far right) with the depiction of a kind of pivoting motion and, like the axes of the four quarters, consist of rays that seem to divide a circle into segments. Like the trigrams of the *Yijing*, they are defined as seven sequential steps and are given primarily as incremental strokes of a line.

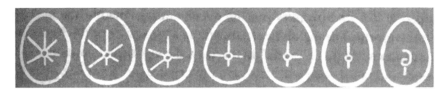

Figure 10.2. The seven stages of the po pilu

We can see that the Chinese concepts and symbols relating to the *Yijing* and the eight trigrams conform in significant ways to the mindset of the plan of cosmology as we understand it to work among other cultures we have explored. Basic Chinese keywords such as *Yijing* are defined as compound terms in much the same way as the name of the Dogon creator-god Amma. In our view, the name Amma expresses the term for the initiating act of biological creation (*am*, referring to "knowledge" in the Biblical sense) tagged to the term for the initiating act of cosmological creation (*maa*, meaning "perception"). As we expect, each Chinese cosmological concept is defined by a word that carries two or more discrete meanings. Groups of related symbols are given in reference to a metaphoric progression (such as the simple act of counting with cardinal numbers, given as a series of stroke-lines) that makes it possible for us to follow and verify their sequential stages. It seems unlikely that what presents itself to us as well-defined parallel elements of a shared cosmological plan could simply be the result of fortuitous coincidence.

11
THE ZODIAC

The concept of the zodiac is one that is found among a variety of cultures from across the globe. It is a complex symbolic form that seems to have taken shape over a long period of time, and an accurate history of its development would make an excellent topic for an extended doctoral dissertation. In practice, it has taken a variety of different forms and typically combines elements drawn from the fields of astronomy, zoology, agriculture, and divination. Many of the symbolic elements contributed by these fields to the practice of the zodiac are documented to have existed in ancient cultures since the advent of writing. However, most researchers credit the invention of the zodiac in its modern form to the Babylonians, and it made its first appearance there in the last few centuries BCE.[1] In China, the origins of the zodiac are traditionally credited, based on mythic references, to the Jade Emperor, Yu Huang.

There is no overt evidence of a zodiac tradition in ancient Egypt until late in its history, during the Ptolemaic era, when the system is thought to have been adopted from the Babylonians by way of the ancient Greeks. Likewise, no overt zodiac tradition is known to exist among the Dogon. However, Marcel Griaule expressed his personal belief in *Conversations with Ogotemmeli* that all of the essential elements that we see combined in the zodiac could be found in the

Dogon creation tradition. In fact, Griaule devotes an entire chapter of his book to the subject, which he titles "The Signs of the Zodiac."[2]

Although the Dogon are a modern-day African tribe, many of the words, symbols, and rituals of Dogon culture bear as close a resemblance to the predynastic tribes as to the early dynastic period of ancient Egypt. Likewise, Dogon society fails to reflect certain practices that are known to have been adopted quite early in Egyptian society, such as the use of a formal system of writing and the observance of the five Egyptian intercalary days, ostensibly used to reconcile their 360-day calendar to a 365-day solar year. Differences such as these suggest that any relationship between the Dogon and the Egyptians must have transpired at a very early point in Egyptian history. The absence of an overt zodiac tradition among the Dogon would be consistent with this view. But consequently, Griaule's observations on how elements of the zodiac exhibit themselves in Dogon culture, taken together with confirming references drawn from the Buddhist stupa cosmology, may constitute our most viable working model for what the various elements of the zodiac may have looked like in ancient China in their earliest forms.

From this perspective, our first clues to how the zodiac symbolism may have derived in China are given by Adrian Snodgrass in *The Symbolism of the Stupa*. Snodgrass suggests that the concept of the four quarters, which we know plays a central role in Chinese cosmology, may serve as a link between the ritual form of the stupa and concepts of the zodiac. This link is expressed in the geometry of the architectural plan of the stupa, which begins with a circle, the figure that is associated with the term *heaven* in China, and culminates in a square, the figure that corresponds to the term *earth* in Chinese cosmology. Recalling that the figure of the circle as it is evoked in the plan of the stupa derives from the progression of shadows cast by the sun each day, Snodgrass tells us that each quarter of the evoked square is associated with three constellations of stars. If we consider all four quarters of the circle as a totality, we can infer symbolic associations in the base plan of the stupa with twelve constellations, and so with the circular stellar layout of the zodiac.

Snodgrass says that it is an expression of these stellar associations that plays out in Chinese architecture as twelve doorways and in the plan of a Chinese city as twelve gates. From a Buddhist perspective, Snodgrass also associates these twelve constellations with the months of the year and with the zodiacal signs. In China, however, the symbolism of the twelve stations of the zodiac is applied somewhat differently, in that it is interpreted to relate symbolically to a repeating cycle of twelve successive Chinese years, rather than to the twelve months of a single year.[3] When we consider the multiple levels of symbolism that characterize other aspects of our plan of cosmology, it seems possible that two symbolic threads may have existed in (or evolved from) the original plan: one given in terms of months and one in terms of years.

We can offer further clarity to these associations through a discussion of similar symbolism as it is defined in relation to the plan of the Dogon granary, an aligned ritual structure that we interpret as an alternate form of the stupa (figure 11.1).

The plan of the Dogon granary evokes a structure that is roughly pyramidal in shape and is characterized by a round base divided into four quarters, a square flat roof, and four flat faces. These four faces are associated with four stars (such as Sirius) or star groups (such as the Pleiades) whose risings and settings regulate the timing of planting and harvesting in the Dogon agricultural calendar. We find similar stellar symbolism associated with the faces of pyramidal structures in regions as far distant as the Americas. This symbolism, which is given as part of an instructed civilizing plan and can be seen as integral to a functioning agriculture, seems to underlie the stellar component of the system of the zodiac.

The plan of the granary provides for eight internal chambers, one associated with each of the grains cultivated by the Dogon tribespeople. These, like the eight trigrams of the *Yijing*, are explicitly said to symbolize eight "seeds" of matter. Four of these chambers are situated on the

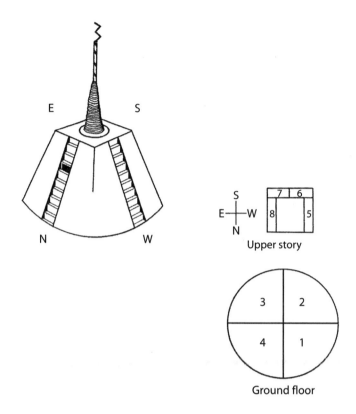

Figure 11.1. Plan of the Dogon granary

ground level of the granary. The plan of these lower chambers would seem to correspond to the four quarters that Wheatley associates with the earliest Chinese cities. The other four chambers are incorporated as part of an upper story of the Dogon granary. Two grains that reside in a cup at the point of intersection of the lower-level partitions symbolize the Dogon creator-god Amma and thereby demonstrate a symbolic relationship to the Dogon egg-in-a-ball figure.

Like a Buddhist stupa, the Dogon granary is understood to symbolize an entire world plan. As such, it includes features that are meant to facilitate the organization of a civilized life. From this perspective, the plan of the Dogon granary also calls for four ten-step staircases, each situated at the center of one of the four faces of the ritual structure.

Each of these staircases is associated conceptually with a class of animals. The western face is associated with insects, the northern face with fish, the southern face with domesticated animals, and the eastern face with birds. These four groupings of living creatures repeat one of the four-stage progressive metaphors that serve to define major categories of symbols in Dogon cosmology. This is similar to the plan for the Chinese zodiac, as seen in figure 11.2.

Figure 11.2. The Chinese zodiac

The steps of the Dogon granary, each of which measures one cubit in depth and one cubit high, define an order of zoologically related animals that are conceptualized as "standing" on one of the steps. When Marcel Griaule, during his initiation to the Dogon creation tradition, expressed mock wonderment at how so many animals could fit on such a small step, the blind priest Ogotemmeli, who was primarily responsible for Griaule's instruction, replied that Griaule should consider these to be "symbolic steps." It was Ogotemmeli's belief that "any number of animals" could fit comfortably on a symbolic step.

The four-step metaphor of Dogon cosmology that correlates stages of creation to conceptual categories of animals provides us with one rationale for interpreting Egyptian deities who are depicted as having animal heads. If by the Dogon metaphor insects correspond to the earliest stages of creation, then it becomes easy to understand why the Egyptian god Kheper, who by our interpretation represents the concept of nonexistence coming into existence, would be portrayed in Egyptian art with the head of a beetle. The same rationale explains why Anubis, who governs the Egyptian underworld, would be depicted with the head of a dog or jackal. Similarly, the symbolism of a deity such as Thoth, who is associated with concepts of writing in Egypt and is portrayed with the head of a bird, represents the symbolic concept of the finished Word and so falls in the last of four progressive categories of creation.

Likewise, as we mentioned in our discussion in *Sacred Symbols of the Dogon* in regard to the cosmological symbolism that is likely to be associated with Egyptian glyph shapes and as we developed in our "Structure of Matter Detail" table in that book, we can see that various stages of matter and cosmological concepts appear to be symbolized by specific animals. Among these we see the owl 🦉, which represents the concept of knowledge, and the fish 🐟, which by our interpretation depicts the processes by which a perceived wave attains mass. We also see the dog or jackal 🐕, which as a scavenger represents the processes of disorder, through which mass in its original wavelike form comes to be reorganized into particles.

Furthermore, in the summer of 2010, just before my friends Egyptologist John Anthony West and geologist Robert Schoch made an exploratory visit to evaluate the ancient megalithic site of Gobekli Tepe in Turkey, which is thought to date to a period around 10,500 BCE, about seven thousand years before the rise of the Egyptian civilization, I made an effort to acquire some understanding of the symbolism of that site. Turning to words and language as a likely point of reference, I learned that there are upward of twenty-five definitions in the Turkish language for the word *tepe* and that at least a dozen of these can be found under a similar pronunciation in the Egyptian hieroglyphic dictionary. I also noticed that many of the animal images that are carved in relief on the megalithic stones of Gobekli Tepe portray animals that have symbolic significance within our plan of cosmology. However, I was perhaps most intrigued with the images of animals that, in my experience, play no obvious cosmological role. Realizing that commonalities of language do seem to exist between modern Turkey and ancient Egypt despite their obvious separation in time by several thousands of years, I decided to look for linguistic clues to the symbolic role played by these animals and so turned to Egyptian dictionary word entries, hoping that a symbolic reading of the names of these animals would offer me some new insight. What I discovered was that each Egyptian animal name was pronounced like an important term of cosmology.

The first implication of this discovery was that it provided me with a rationale by which to possibly explain the images on the megaliths. The Gobekli Tepe site dates to a time long before the first surviving evidence of any organized system of writing, which does not appear until around 3000 BCE. Gobekli Tepe is located in the same region in which the earliest historical evidence of cultivated grains is found, along with—somewhat later—the earliest known examples of metallurgy. Each of these practices constitutes an instructed skill associated with the Dogon civilizing plan. The megalithic stones at Gobekli Tepe offer perhaps the earliest example of skilled stone masonry, which is yet another of the civilizing skills associated with the Dogon plan.

If we accept the view of the Dogon priests that civilizing concepts, tagged to their system of cosmology, were deliberately taught to humanity in ancient times, then the concurrence of these same skills in the vicinity of Gobekli Tepe could suggest that a much earlier attempt at civilizing instruction had been made. I knew that this possibility was supported by the documented belief in ancient Egypt in a mythical First Time, which was referred to as Zep Tepi. If our supposition were true, then the animal images found on the Gobekli Tepe megaliths could represent a very early type of protowriting, set down mnemonically in the images of animals. We can imagine that a hunter-gatherer would see the image of a familiar animal carved into the megalith, say its name aloud, and in so doing speak an important term of cosmology.

From that point forward for the inductee, any sightings of that animal in the wild would serve to reinforce the related cosmological concept for the hunter-gatherer, in much the same way that the daily acts of Dogon life serve to reinforce the teachings of their creation tradition. The idea that cosmological concepts were tagged to animal images is one that became apparent from our earliest investigations of ancient Egyptian glyph images. It seemed reasonable that the animal symbols pictured in the Chinese zodiac might also have cosmological import.

The Chinese term for zodiac is *shengxiao;* it is again a compound term, one that combines the words *sheng* and *xiao.* The word *sheng* implies "cosmic," a term that comes from a Greek word that means "order."[4] The word *sheng* is a likely correlate to the Egyptian word *skhem,* which refers to "divine power" or the "power of nature."[5] Based on their common multiple meanings, we associate this word *sheng* with the phonetic root *saqa,* which means "to set in strict order."[6] The Chinese word *xiao* can mean "little" or "resemblance." In our previous discussion of the Sage King Fu-xi in chapter 3, we already correlated the Chinese root *xi* to the Egyptian word *skhai,* which means "to celebrate a festival," and to the Dogon word Sigi, which is the name of the important Dogon festival celebration. The Egyptian word *skhai* forms the likely root of the word *skhen,* which means "little." It also corresponds to the phonetic root *skah,* which means "to call to mind a person or thing," which we take as a working definition of the concept of resemblance. Based on these meanings together, we interpret the combined Chinese term *shengxiao* to convey the notion of "cosmic resemblance," which on one level is what the zodiac system appears to symbolically represent.

In support of these tentative correlations we note that the Chinese

word *sheng* can also designate a musical sound. A likely Egyptian counterpart, *sekh,* means "to strike a lyre," thereby making a musical sound.
A homonym for this same Egyptian word means "to make to be," which
is a definition that relates directly to the notion of creation.[7]

Budge tells us that the Egyptian word *skhai* can also mean "to make
rise up or appear," terms that are used in Dogon cosmology to describe
how the structure of matter is evoked from waves.[8] So based on our
comparative references, the Chinese name for the zodiac would seem to
refer to a set of symbols that pertain to the concept of cosmic order, and
more specifically to little things within the cosmic order that rise up and
appear, such as particles, and larger things that rise, like stars and constellations. This would again place the symbolism reflected by the term for
zodiac squarely in the realm of the initial stages of the creation of matter.

When we explore Egyptian words for the animals depicted in the
Chinese zodiac, we see ongoing evidence of a symbolic theme that relates
to stages in the growth of matter. Just as we found with the Gobekli
Tepe animals, the Egyptian names for each animal depicted in the
Chinese zodiac take their roots from a phonetic value that has apparent
significance within our system of cosmology. For example, the Egyptian
word for hare or rabbit is *unun*. This word is based on the phonetic root
un, which means "to exist," and is the name of the Egyptian god of existence.[9] The word *un* is written with glyphs that represent two types of
vibration: the nest glyph ⌖, which we take as the image of an electron
orbit, and the wave glyph ∿, which in our view, as we mentioned in
chapter 7, represents the vibratory pattern of a wave. Because it is often
not the animal names themselves but rather the root phonetic values on
which they are based that express the cosmological concept that seems
to be symbolized, the interpretations given here are necessarily indirect
ones. However, the notion that the Egyptian animals symbolize stages
of matter is upheld by the symbolic form of the Egyptian word for animal itself, which Budge gives as *aa-t*. Symbolically the word reads "that
which ⌇ comes to be 𓄛 mass/matter ◠," followed by the cosmic egg
glyph 𓏴. The cosmic egg, of course, represents one of the primordial

sources of matter; it is the repository that is thought to have held all the potential seeds of the future universe before the big bang. This same glyph is also the Egyptian symbol for Sirius, the star that is often associated with the teachers of our ancient civilizing plan.

From this perspective, and based on the symbolism of the Egyptian phonetic roots on which their names are based, the animals presented in the Chinese zodiac can be seen to symbolize progressive stages in the formation of matter:

The dog is a Chinese symbol associated with the cosmic egg and so makes an appropriate starting point for zodiac animal symbolism. The Chinese god Pangu is a dog deity who wakes up and emerges from the cosmic egg. In Egypt, the term Sothis, which represents Sirius, the Dog Star, is associated with the same figure that is used by the Dogon to represent the cosmic egg ⋀. The Egyptian word for "dog" is *auau* (a phonetic value that is likely based on the sound of a dog's bark) and represents the "raising up" of matter. This is a process that we compared to the shape of a tent's peak ^ in chapter 7. In this instance, the likely symbolism is to the very similar "v" shape that is made by a dog's mouth when the animal opens it to bark.[10]

The pig, whose Egyptian name is *apeh,* represents the initial appearance of space. Symbolically, the word reads "that which is ⎰ space ⬚ twists and pivots ⦦," followed by the pig glyph .[11]

The rat, whose Egyptian name is *penu,* represents the growth of the precursors of matter. Symbolically, the word reads "space ⬚ vibrates ∿ and particles ○ grow ," followed by a glyph that symbolizes the emanation and growth of matter ⦦ and three stacked seeds that we take to represent particles.[12]

The ox, represented by the Egyptian name *aua,* symbolizes the concept of the manifestation or emergence of the components of matter. This same meaning is also associated with the horns of any animal ⋃, which convey a sense of "rising upward." This meaning is conveyed symbolically in terms of the growth of a plant in the word *aua,* which reads "that which 〔 grows upward 〕," followed by the ox glyph .[13]

The tiger has no word entry in Budge's *An Egyptian Hieroglyphic Dictionary.* However, we know that the tiger is a powerful animal that can cover distances quickly. So one presumption, based both on the context of the symbol within the structure of matter and on the attributes of the animal, is that this animal may symbolize the notion of space growing and vibration quickening. However, there is alternate symbolism that could be associated with the tiger's stripes. The meaning of "stripe" is associated with the Egyptian word *uben,* whose glyphs refer to "the rayed place of the growth of matter."[14] We take this as a likely reference to the growth of the egg of the world, whose vibrations are characterized as seven rays of a star.

The rabbit or hare is represented by the Egyptian word *unt.* As we mentioned in chapter 10, this animal is taken to represent the concept of vibration within the egg of the world, which we take as a counterpart to the Calabi-Yau space in string theory. Again, this symbolic association is based on a hare's observable tendency to twitch.

The dragon is another term that is not found in Budge's dictionary. Context suggests that this creature represents the seven winding vibrations of the spiraling egg of the world. Appropriately, the dragon holds the seventh place among our progression of animals depicted in the Chinese zodiac.

The snake represents the completed egg of the world, which defines the Dogon concept of the Word of matter. In Dogon cosmology, the notion of the completed egg spans the seventh and the eighth stages of the egg of the world, the stages in which it comes to completion, is pierced by its final ray, and the Word of matter is spoken. Appropriately, the snake is the eighth animal in our zodiac progression. Budge assigns the phonetic value of "tch" to this glyph, which forms the root of the words *tchet-t,* meaning "word," and *tchet,* meaning "to speak, to say."[15] The completion of mass or matter is accompanied by the overt appearance of gravity—the force that bends mass. The Egyptian word for "snake" is *aar-t.* Symbolically it reads "that which is ⟨ the force ⟂ that bends/warps ⌣ mass △."[16] In Buddhism, the serpent also symbolizes the concept of the completion of matter, in the sense that the final undulations of the serpent represent the point at which time becomes fixed and matter is established.[17]

The horse is identified by the Egyptian word *semsem,* which derives from the phonetic root *sem,* meaning "form" or "image." A homonym for this same word means "to collect, to heap together." Symbolically, the suggestion is that the horse represents matter that collects together to form small particles.[18] In Buddhism, the horse plays a symbolic role in relation to aligned ritual structures that would seem to symbolize the first overt manifestation of matter. From the perspective of Dogon symbolism, four-legged animals are associated with the third stage of matter, the stage that would immediately precede our visible world.[19]

The sheep, appropriately enough, goes by the Egyptian word *ba.* Budge lists a homonym for this word that means "to pay homage," which can be read symbolically as "spirit 𓅽 raised up 𓀢." The implication is that the sheep represents the growth of mass to form larger particles of matter.[20]

The monkey, whose Egyptian name is *kenmut,* represents the concept of larger particles of matter fully formed. This word is based on the phonetic root *kenem,* which means "to break forth," in the sense of "coming into existence."

The rooster is yet another animal for which there is no Egyptian dictionary entry. However, we know based on the Dogon four-stage animal-kingdom metaphor that, as a bird, it symbolizes a concept that relates to the fourth and final stage of matter. The Egyptian counterpart to the atom-like po of the Dogon is expressed by the word *pau-t,* which Budge tells us refers to "mass" or "matter" and defines the flying goose glyph . The obvious symbolic characteristic of a rooster is the loud crowing sound it makes. If the final stage of the Second World of matter is characterized as the spoken Word, then it seems sensible that the final stage of the Third World of matter would be represented by an animal whose crowing could symbolize the speaking of that Word.

12
THE COSMOLOGICAL ROLE OF THE TURTLE

Symbolic relationships between animals and concepts of cosmology are evident from the earliest eras of the traditions we have studied, and the zodiac, as discussed in the prior chapter, can be seen as an outgrowth of that symbology. There is one animal in particular that seems to have been pivotal to ancient Chinese concepts of creation but is not emphasized in Africa, Egypt, India, or Tibet and is also not overtly included among the animals of the Chinese zodiac, and that is the turtle. But on closer examination we realize that the turtle's likely relationship to the zodiac may be comparable to Neith's relationship to the eight paired deities of the Egyptian Ennead or Ogdoad, whose emergence mimics the divisions of a fertilized egg during the processes of biological reproduction. The divisions of an egg occur inside a womb, and it seems reasonable to assign that womb to the mother goddess. The layout of the zodiac closely resembles the circular configuration of a turtle's shell, and so it makes sense to infer that the turtle provided a framework for the conceptual design. From that perspective, like Neith the turtle is "in the picture," only too large to be recognized based on our perspective.

We'll see in this chapter how the concept of the turtle is one that bears a complex relationship to Chinese mythology, cosmology, and practices of divination. Mythic references make it certain that associations between the turtle and ancient cosmology are based on what was a very ancient identification, and not on more recent Chinese scholarly interpretation.[1] By the time of the Shang dynasty, one practice of divination was to induce cracks in the outward side of turtle shells by applying fire to internal hollows in the shell. China scholars are not yet certain how these cracks may have been read. Many of the earliest oracle bone writings constitute commentary, which was carved into the inner sides of the shell, on the prophetic meanings that were interpreted to have been conveyed by these cracks.[2] These interpretations typically concerned whether an upcoming event would be fortuitous or ominous, and sometimes foretold the likely timing of those events.

In China, the turtle is also intimately associated with concepts of creation and plays a significant role in Chinese cosmology. Cosmological references to the turtle date from the time of the mother goddess Nu-wa, and so the turtle can be said to rank among the earliest Chinese symbols. The concept of the turtle or tortoise in Chinese cosmology may relate to the primordial Vedic deity Kasyapa, the father of the devas, whose name means "tortoise" and who symbolizes the universe.[3]

One ancient Chinese myth tells of how, after the foundations of the Earth crumbled, Nu-wa cut off the four legs of a turtle and used them as pillars to prop up the sky.[4] This myth reinforces cosmological symbolism that associates the domed shape of the turtle shell with the concept of the cosmos. The hemispheric shape of the turtle shell is interpreted in Chinese cosmology as combining the dome of the sky with the flatness of the Earth. This interpretation restates a previously discussed notion that associates the concept of heaven or sky with the circle and the concept of Earth with a square. The figure of a hemisphere symbolically reconciles those two concepts. The hollows of the underside shell of the turtle are also associated symbolically in China with the concept of water.

This same symbolism is upheld in the Dogon tradition, where, as Griaule and Dieterlen tell us, the turtle is one of the representations of the world. The hemispheric shell represents the celestial world (heaven or sky), while the "belly" of the turtle represents the Earth.[5]

We can expand on this symbolism by noting that the dome is a three-dimensional representation of the hemisphere shape ⌒, a figure that we already correlate in our cosmologies to the concept of mass or matter and to the symbolic term *earth*. We also know that, from a scientific perspective, the processes of creation do, in fact, work to separate space from mass or matter, much as Chinese mythic symbolism suggests that their purpose is to separate sky from earth. Likewise, we can see the actions taken during the act of divination as a symbolic repetition of the steps by which mass is evoked within the cosmology. Fire (which in our view is symbolic of an act of perception) is applied to the hollow of the underside shell of a turtle (symbolic of water or waves) to produce cracks in the outer side of the turtle shell (symbolic of the differentiated particles of matter).

The written glyphs that compose the Egyptian word for turtle, along with the cosmological symbolism of the animals that we discussed in chapter 11 in terms of the zodiac, support the view that the turtle symbolizes the cosmological concept of mass. This interpretation is also upheld by the written form of the Egyptian word *shet*, which means "turtle" and which in our view constitutes a defining word for the turtle glyph 🐢. Symbolically, the word *shet* reads "reserved or preserved ⟨⟩ mass ⌒," followed by the turtle glyph 🐢. Another Egyptian word based on this same phonetic root is pronounced "shta-t." It refers to a "mystery" or "something hidden." According to Budge, one of the spellings of the word for turtle refers to "those whose arms are hidden." From a symbolic standpoint, it is easy to see how a turtle (an animal that can retract its legs inside its shell) would come to symbolize the concept of something hidden and how, given the Egyptian glyph symbolism, the hemispheric shape of a turtle would make it a likely avatar for hidden mass or matter. Budge tells us that this same phonetic value, *shen*, was used as a title for the hidden god Amen, who was the Egyptian counterpart to the Dogon creator-god Amma and whose name can also mean "hidden." The Dogon priests explicitly associate Amma with mythological processes by which matter is created.

One of the instructed concepts that is said to have been introduced to humanity through the Dogon civilizing plan is the notion of clothing. In China (again based on symbolism that seems fairly obvious) the shell of the turtle also symbolizes the concept of clothing. On a somewhat darker level, the turtle is associated in China with the belief that the spirit of a person who dies essentially sheds his or her body and leaves it behind, much as if it were clothing. So, from this perspective, it makes sense that the Egyptian word *shet-t*, or *shta*, refers to a "covering, shroud, garment." In this same vein, another Egyptian word, *shet*, also refers to the cloth bandages that are used to swathe a mummy.[6]

This same death-related symbolism offers us an explanation for why the Egyptian word *shet* also refers to the concepts of "grief, sorrow" and to the meaning "to rend, to tear." Mourners of a dead person in some ancient traditions such as Judaism expressed their grief symbolically by physically rending or tearing a garment. This symbolism might also possibly relate to an Egyptian death ritual called the opening of the mouth, in which a hole is cut in the cloth bandages that are used to wrap and enclose a mummy. From a cosmological perspective, these wrapped bandages call to mind the spiraling stages of the Dogon egg of the world, which are described as rays of a star of increasing length. This egg is not considered to be complete until the seventh ray grows long enough to actually pierce the egg, an event that is compared by the Dogon priests to the "death" of the egg. Death symbolism that relates to the term *shet* is also underscored by the Egyptian word *shtai-t*, which means "shrine, coffin, sarcophagus," and by the word *shta-t*, which refers to a vulture, a scavenger animal that feeds on dead carcasses.

By the time of the Han dynasty in China, the region beneath the earth was said to be populated by dragons, turtles, and fishlike creatures. This outlook takes on a more sensible aspect when we consider it in terms of the attributes of these animals that lend themselves to cosmological symbolism.[7] The concept of an underworld is the domain of the dead in ancient Egypt and one that we associate with the Dogon Second World of matter—the world in which matter in its wavelike form is disrupted, then reorganized and transformed by way of spiraling structures into discrete particles. It is this same spiraling process of transformation that we propose was symbolized by the coiled dragon of the Chinese zodiac and that the Dogon priests assign to their concept of the nummo fish. As we noted in *Sacred Symbols of the Dogon*, the nummo fish "stands literally at the doorway to the creation efforts of the god Amma at the point where matter unfolds." Based on these and other references, our interpretation is that the turtle represents the product of these transformations and therefore would also correspond to the scientific concept of mass.

In the Chinese myth mentioned earlier in this chapter, in which the mother goddess Nu-wa appropriates the four legs of the turtle and uses them as pillars to prop up the sky, it seems significant that these pillars are specifically said not to have been placed—as we might expect—at the four cardinal points of east, north, west, and south. Instead, she places them midway between the cardinal points, as if to create four more points on a compass by which to mark the directions of northeast, northwest, southwest, and southeast. Sarah Allen suggests that these placements match the orientation of the four feet of a living turtle in relation to its head and tail. In fact, the markings on a turtle's underside bear a resemblance to the axis lines that serve to differentiate the segments of a circle or an oval. The four endpoints of these axes—in combination with the four legs of the turtle—and an implied center-point (which is also understood to be directional) define nine directions and so can be seen to repeat the basic symbolism of ancient land division in China. With a little imagination, the configuration of the underside of the turtle can also be seen to mimic the traditional plan of the Chinese city itself (figure 12.1).[8]

Through cross-cultural comparisons and the Egyptian root phonetic value of *shet,* we can link the seemingly distinct threads of Chinese

Figure 12.1. The underside of a turtle shell

and Egyptian symbolism that relate to the turtle: one that pertains to cosmology, another to concepts of the underworld such as death and mourning, and another to the wrapping and preservation of a mummy. Once again, this same set of symbolic themes comes together in Dogon descriptions of the egg of the world. In our studies, we have previously compared this Dogon concept of a primordial egg with its rays to a related drawing—the Egyptian star-in-circle glyph ⊕ that represents the Egyptian Tuat, or underworld. Budge tells us that Shetu is the name of a "great god" whose symbolism is to "the eight morning stars." These stars compose what Budge calls "the constellation of the Tortoise." Astronomically, this refers to a group of eight stars that surround the star Vega. However from a cosmological perspective, the reference is likely to be to the same eight vibrations that we associate with the creation of matter. Symbolically the name Shetu reads "preservation given," followed by the star glyph ✶ (representing the number five) and three strokes-lines ||| (representing the number three). Taken together, the trailing glyphs of the name convey the number eight, which we take as a symbolic reference both to the eight stars of the constellation and to the eight stages of vibration of matter.

It seems likely from our discussion of the symbolism of the turtle that, from a cosmological standpoint, it represents the concept of mass or matter. Would it not then also seem sensible to use a symbolic image of mass (the turtle shell; figure 12.2) as the basic pattern for a figure that is meant to present each of the major component stages in the formation of matter?

Figure 12.2. The turtle's shell

13
ORACLE BONE
WRITING

The earliest inscriptions that are officially recognized as examples of ancient Chinese writing are attributed to the Shang dynasty and date to around 1300 BCE according to some sources, or to as early as 1500 BCE according to others—approximately the same period as is estimated for the earliest hieroglyphic writings of the Na-khi. These Shang-dynasty inscriptions, which are referred to as oracle bone script, were composed of characters that were scratched into the neck bones (scapulae) of oxen and, as we noted in chapter 12, on the inner sides of turtle shells.[1] Some authorities interpret these writings to have been primarily concerned with acts of divination and meant to forecast favorable and unfavorable future events.[2] These divination rituals were practiced by early Chinese shamans and are believed by some authorities to have provided a foundation for Daoism.[3] Other researchers credit the development of this earliest Chinese writing form to an abrupt and poorly understood imperative to record and keep astronomical records, which are also found similarly inscribed in bone.[4]

As an important aspect of other cosmological comparisons, I devoted an entire chapter of *The Cosmological Origins of Myth and Symbol* to a discussion of the written hieroglyphic language of the Dongba priests of the Na-khi tribe.[5] In that chapter, I focused on phonetic and symbolic parallels that are found between a number of Egyptian glyph shapes and outwardly similar glyphs of the Na-khi. As we work to carry these comparisons forward yet another step to the ancient Chinese oracle bone writings, we should emphasize that the academic uncertainties that surround these earliest Chinese inscriptions render any observations we might make about them necessarily speculative.

Language scholars acknowledge that aspects of the later Chinese hieroglyphic language seem to have been influenced by both the oracle bone inscriptions and the early Na-khi system of writing, which itself seems to reflect influences that were likely drawn from India and Mongolia.[6] However, I argued in *The Cosmological Origins of Myth and Symbol* that some of the Na-khi references that are thought possibly to be of Mongolian origin, such as the distinctly non-Chinese phonetic values that are represented in some names on ancient Na-khi lists of mythical kings, may actually reflect the influence of a common cosmology, not influences from Mongolia.

Similarities between the oracle bone inscriptions and later Chinese systems of writing contributed significantly to our ability to read the oracle bone inscriptions. The oracle bone inscriptions provide examples of approximately 4,500 glyph shapes, as compared with the roughly 4,000 characters of the Egyptian hieroglyphic language. This number is far less than the perhaps 80,000 Chinese hieroglyphic characters. Figure 13.1 offers side-by-side comparisons of a number of oracle bone

Figure 13.1. Oracle bone glyph shapes compared to Chinese glyphs

glyph shapes with likely glyph correlates from later written Chinese language, along with their interpreted meanings.

Researchers who are familiar with the many ancient written texts of the Na-khi say that topics relating to cosmology were central to this body of writings. Some go so far as to say that the Na-khi system of writing was developed primarily to record their cosmological traditions. Like ancient Egyptian texts, the writings of the Na-khi involved two distinct scripts: one that was phonetic in nature and one that was pictographic. Like the Egyptian hieroglyphs, the Na-khi pictographic words omit written vowel sounds—a characteristic that we view as a signature of our plan of cosmology—and often include glyphs that are not vocalized. Joseph Francis Charles Rock, author of the two-part *A Na-Khi–English Encyclopedic Dictionary,* and a leading authority on Na-khi culture and language, describes a rebus-like approach to interpreting these pictograms that agrees with the alternative method we proposed in our symbolic approach to the reading of Egyptian hieroglyphic words.

The close matches we find, in both form and symbolism, among the sun glyph characters as they appear in the oracle bone writings, in the ancient Egyptian hieroglyphic language, and in the hieroglyphic writings of the Na-khi support two of our central suppositions: first, that many of the earliest symbols of written language seem to have been adopted from an already-existing cosmology, and second, that the cosmologies of these ancient cultures followed what appears to be a common plan. The sun glyph symbol is a shape that is quite recognizable (figure 13.2), even in the squared form it takes in later Chinese language. In each of these cultures, this glyph is associated with the same set of well-defined cosmological concepts.

The sun glyph as it appears in the Na-khi tradition, with its axial division into four segments, displays features of the egg-in-a-ball figure from Dogon cosmology and also could convey the concept of four quarters that we know lies at the heart of ancient Chinese cosmology. The symbolism of the figure, which can represent the sun and the concept of

Figure 13.2. Sun glyph shapes: oracle bone (left), Egyptian (middle), and Na-khi (right)

a day, and its use in various words of each culture to express concepts of time, may positively link it to the open form of the Egyptian and oracle bone sun glyphs, because the Na-khi symbol for the sun is divided by intersecting axis lines or rays, while their symbol for a day is not. The figures are also linked to our cosmology by way of the geometry of the aligned ritual shrines, which evokes the same figure. This link is supported in all three cultures through the use of the cubit, the common unit of measure by which alignment of each of these structures was facilitated. These attributes of the sun glyph figure—taken all on their own—encompass a fairly broad range of arguments that support our outlook on ancient cosmology and language.

As we take a closer look at various inscribed characters of the oracle bone writings, other resemblances become apparent that could also be of cosmological significance, especially when considered in light of their similarity to various well-defined cosmological drawings of the Dogon and cosmologically related Egyptian glyphs. Perhaps the first and most obvious of these is the oracle bone glyph that is traditionally understood to symbolize the concept of nothingness. We can see in figure 13.3 that the figure depicted by the glyph is that of a person whose arms and hands are spread apart and separated from one another. This image compares symbolically to the Egyptian glyph that represents the concept of negation, as expressed by the term *not.* Like the oracle bone figure, the meaning of the Egyptian glyph is also conveyed through the image of arms and hands that are spread apart and separated, and so the two can be seen to reflect a similar expressional mind-set.

Figure 13.3. Glyphs that represent nothingness or negation. The figure at left is the oracle bone figure symbolizing "nothingness," and the figure at right is the Egyptian glyph for "negation."

Another quite recognizable figure is presented in figure 13.4: the oracle bone fish glyph (left), which displays a number of details that have cosmological importance to the Dogon priests. This glyph is a likely counterpart to the Dogon nummo fish drawing (right), a figure that, as it is explained in Dogon cosmology, is central to the processes of the creation of matter. Based partly on the context of creation in which the nummo fish drawing is given, the figure seems meant to illustrate the same initial transformations of matter as are described symbolically by the seven stages of Daoism and by conceptual terms we have related to the term Yijing and the Chinese zodiac.

The suggestion is that the nummo fish graphically depicts a series of microcosmic events that transpire after an initial act of perception disturbs matter as it exists in its primordial wavelike state. This act of perception disrupts the original perfect order of the wave and initiates a process that effectively reorganizes the wave into what we perceive as particles of matter. Based on this scenario we interpret the lined tail of the nummo fish drawing to represent the wavelike source of matter and the central dot within the body of the fish to represent the point of disruption that is created by the act of perception. The corresponding oracle bone glyph arguably displays both of these elements. If we use the terminology of the Dogon priests, the upward-pointing "V"

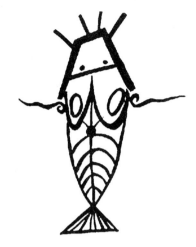

Figure 13.4. The oracle bone fish glyph (left) and the Dogon nummo fish drawing (right) show a number of similarities.

of the nummo fish drawing depicts mass that is drawn upward like a tent. This upward motion causes the waves on either side of the tent to vibrate and induces them to encircle or pivot. We see a similar upward "V" shape in the oracle bone glyph.

The diagonal line of the nummo fish drawing that slants upward and to the right to separate the head from the body represents a conceptual division between the Dogon First World of matter (matter that exists as waves) and the Dogon Second World (where matter is reordered as fundamental particles). A similar upward-slanting line appears in the oracle bone glyph. The two dots that appear above this line in the nummo fish drawing represent a pair of fundamental particles of matter. We see a similar dot above the line in the oracle bone glyph. The squared, pyramid-like head shape of the nummo fish represents the concept of mass and is conceptually similar to the curved, hemisphere-like head of the oracle bone glyph—the same shape that we interpret to symbolize mass or matter in the Egyptian hieroglyphic language. The two fins on opposing sides of the nummo fish call to mind membranes that are the by-product of the vibrations of matter in string theory. The oracle bone fish glyph displays two comparable fins. The parallel nature of the two figures suggests that they were meant to symbolize matching concepts in the two cosmologies.

Resemblances can be seen between other symbolic shapes in the oracle bone script and those from the various cosmologies we have studied. For example, in figure 13.5, the oracle bone moon glyph (left), although it is rotated in its relative orientation, presents a similar image to the moon glyph as it is written in the ancient Egyptian hieroglyphic language (right).

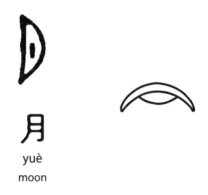

yuè
moon

Figure 13.5. The oracle bone moon glyph (left) and the Egyptian moon glyph (right) also are quite similar. Also shown is the later Chinese counterpart to the Oracle Bone moon glyph.

Similarly, in figure 13.6, the oracle bone glyph that is interpreted to represent a child (left) takes the same basic form as the Egyptian ankh glyph (right), which is traditionally understood as a symbol for life.

In figure 13.7, we also see that the oracle bone field glyph (left), which may call to mind the groups of square plots of land that are characteristic of the ancient well-field system, takes a form that is outwardly similar to the Egyptian field glyph (right).

Similarly, in figure 13.8, the oracle bone mountain glyph (left) presents a very close match for the Egyptian glyph that is traditionally interpreted to represent a hill, mountain, or horizon (right).

Each of the preceding glyph comparisons demonstrates the very similar ways in which symbolic meaning came to be reflected in the

zi

child

Figure 13.6. The form of the oracle bone child glyph (left) is similar to that of the Egyptian ankh glyph (right), which represents life.

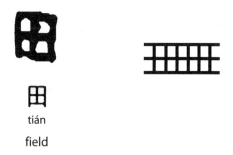

tián

field

Figure 13.7. The oracle bone field glyph (left) is similar to the Egyptian field glyph (right).

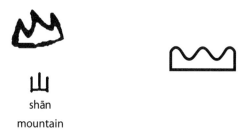

shān

mountain

Figure 13.8. The oracle bone mountain glyph (left) is similar to the Egyptian hill or mountain glyph (right).

characters of the earliest written languages of ancient China, Tibet, Egypt, and Africa. The strikingly similar mode of expression that is apparent from culture to culture reflects a common mind-set about how symbolic meaning was conceived of and conveyed. The glyphs themselves give tangible expression to many of the same resemblances we have previously discussed in relation to other aspects of the cosmologies of these same regions. Also, because many of these shapes play well-defined symbolic roles in the Dogon, Egyptian, and Buddhist cosmologies—and are often tagged to the same symbolic meanings in those cosmologies—the examples also uphold our belief that symbolic shapes and meanings from a preexisting cosmology were adopted as early written characters within these languages. Furthermore, the matched shape-and-concept pairings in both the written languages and the cosmologies would seem to preclude simple coincidence as an explanation for the resemblances. The suggestion, again, is that these cultures came to written language by way of a common source or point of reference—namely, cosmology.

14
SYMBOLISM OF THE
GER, OR YURT

The Chinese, Mongolian, Siberian, and Turkish cultures are home to a traditional structure called a *ger,* or a yurt, which could have potential significance for our study of cosmology. A yurt is a kind of portable dwelling or tent supported by poles and covered with felt or animal hides (figure 14.1). Like other terms that relate to cosmology, the word *yurt* can carry multiple meanings, and like many ancient Chinese concepts, it is assigned differing origins depending on the source referenced. Some say that the word *yurt* derives from a Russian root, others that the word is Turkish, while the Pakistani word *ger* and the similar Hindi term *ghar* seem to be more ancient names for the structure. Most sources agree that the term *yurt* can refer to the concept of a dwelling or a household, to the place or location where a yurt is built, and to the yurt structure itself, while some say that it also implies the concept of homeland. In the Kazakh and Uyghur languages, the structure is known by the term *kiyiz uy,* meaning "felt house." Afghans traditionally refer to the yurt with the words *kherga* or *jirga.*[1] The northern indigenous people of Russia and the Chaplino Eskimos make use of a mobile yurt-like structure that they call a *yaranga.*

Some authorities, such as *National Geographic* magazine, state without reservation that yurt use in Siberia and Asia is thousands of years old.[2]

Figure 14.1. A yurt

However, like many of the other cosmological forms and concepts of China we have discussed, definitive evidence by which to date the development and use of the yurt has not been established to the satisfaction of all researchers. Siberian carvings that may represent yurts have been dated to the Bronze Age, which would be roughly contemporaneous with our cosmology. Likewise, firsthand accounts from ancient travelers such as Herodotus seem to document the use of yurts in the late centuries BCE, but some scholars feel that these descriptions could be subject to alternate interpretation. Consequently, the earliest unequivocal documentation of the use of these dwellings in Asia may only date to the time of Genghis Khan, from around 1100 CE. Evidence shows the invention of yurts in Turkey to have possibly occurred as early as the fourth century BCE. One group of researchers cites a depiction on an engraved bronze bowl as evidence of the yurt's existence in Iran as early as 600 BCE.[3]

Although the traditional yurt is a round structure and so would not seem to lend itself to the principle of cardinal alignment that characterizes many of the aligned structures in our cosmologies, the inner structure of the yurt centers on four wooden poles that are, in fact, typically aligned to the four cardinal points. Based on this suggestive detail, if we were to pursue further symbolic resemblances between a yurt and a Buddhist stupa, we would expect to find that the round geometry of the yurt in some way represents the sun. As it turns out, the round upper section of the yurt is traditionally understood to symbolize the sun. The opening entry to a yurt is traditionally aligned to the south, and the directions of west and east are associated with the cosmological concepts of yin and yang—directions that are also symbolically associated with the concepts of male and female, respectively. Mongolian symbolism associates the four cardinal directions of the yurt with primordial elements. We take each of these symbolic elements to be signature characteristics of a stupa.

The center of the yurt is the location where a fire—and sometimes an altar—is built. The altar takes the form of a square that is marked out at the center of the circular structure, and so it can be seen to facilitate the symbolic squaring of a circle. The column of smoke that rises from the fire, which symbolically marks a vertical axis, is associated with the cosmological concept of a world tree, much as the axis mundi that defines the center point of a stupa is associated with the tree of life in the Dogon and Buddhist cosmologies.

Other traditional symbols that attend the plan of the yurt are also largely anticipated by our model of cosmology. For example, like the base plan of a stupa, the yurt form is generally understood to represent a sacred circle associated with the sun. The ritual act of raising a yurt— much like the act of building a stupa—is interpreted to symbolize the bringing of order to chaos. Like the Dogon granary, the architectural plan of the yurt is defined in terms of a round base that rises to a flat roof. Also, similar to the plan of an ancient Chinese city that defines a center at the point of intersection of its two axes, the yurt is considered to represent the center of the cosmological universe, or macrocosm. However, again in favorable comparison to the Dogon granary and the stupa, the yurt structure is also understood to contain within itself the essence of matter as it exists in the microcosm. The underside of its curved roof is said to reflect the "vault of the heaven," a phrase that is often associated in various cosmological myths with the process of the separation of earth and sky.

In Mongolia the yurt structure can be referred to as a *hooghan* or a *tiipii*. When we examine the developmental forms of the yurt, as seen in figure 14.2, we see that the earliest of its forms presents essentially the same structure as a Native American tepee, as might be inferred from the similar Mongolian term. The second and third stages of yurt development bear an outward resemblance to the Buddhist stupa and the Dogon granary. The fourth and perhaps classic form of a yurt closely resembles the Navajo round house in North America, which is traditionally called a hogan. Once again, the similar Mongolian term invites the supposition of a relationship between the two forms. Meanwhile, the term *hogan* itself, which is similar to *hogon,* the title given to a Dogon priest, offers yet another point of intersection between the yurt concept and the ancient system of cosmology we have been actively pursuing.

The structural and symbolic similarities that can be shown to exist between a Native American tepee and a yurt may uphold the views of some researchers who believe that migrations occurred in ancient times from Asia into North America. Theorists propose that the ancestors of some Native American tribes traveled across the Bering Strait into North America as recently as five thousand years ago. Proponents of these theories cite a wide range of linguistic and cultural similarities that are evident between various Native American tribes and modern inhabitants of Tibet, Siberia, Mongolia, and China. Likewise, genetic studies have been conducted with some Native American tribes whose

Figure 14.2. Evolution of a ger, *or yurt*

results suggest that several different migrations may have occurred independently from one another, some originating in Asia and at least one in Central or South America. The physical resemblances between some members of the Navajo tribe and modern-day Tibetans can at times be so striking that observers sometime claim to be unable to distinguish between the two.[4] One article on the subject of these genetic studies, titled "DNA Analysis on Native Americans," states:

> The first research on living Native American tribes showed they were composed of four distinct mtDNA haplogroups called A, B, C, and D. This means that the Native Americans are derived from four different lineages. These haplogroups were also found in native populations in Central and South America. . . . Three of these haplogroups, A, C, and D [,] are found primarily in Siberian Asia.[5]

Broader concepts of cosmology as they relate to the yurt form, for both the Siberian and Native American tribes, also align favorably with the plan of cosmology we have been pursuing. In both, the universe is conceived of as existing in three worlds, comparable in a general way to the three conceptual worlds of matter as they are defined in Dogon cosmology. The circular top of a yurt represents the gateway to an upper world, calling to mind the Dogon Third World of matter, and is called the *tono*, a term that is also applied to the third conceptual category of matter in Dogon cosmology. One traditional belief is that a shaman either climbs the world tree or his spirit ascends upward through this opening in the yurt and, by doing so, he is transformed into a bird. Such imagery recalls Dogon symbolism that assigns the fourth and final stage in the creation of matter to the concept of birds.[6] This dome-shaped section of a yurt that represents the uppermost level of creation is reminiscent of the hemisphere or dome that we associate with the concept of mass or matter in our related cosmologies. The symbolic attributes of a ger, or yurt, are consistent for all cultural groups throughout Mongolia, where—like the

Dogon granary and Buddhist stupa—the structure is understood to embody the symbolism of an entire worldview.

In light of the many correlations we see in structure and symbolism between the yurt and the aligned stupa and granary, it seems completely reasonable to view the yurt as a kind temporary or mobile stupa. At first blush, the need for such a structure would seem to go against the very mind-set of a creation tradition and cultural plan that seems to have been studiously designed for longevity. It is this same sense of longevity that was reflected in the three-thousand-year history of the ancient Egyptian culture and the presumably five-thousand-year history of the Dogon, and that underlies the very notion of the construction of a megalithic structure such as a stone pyramid. Then again, the concept of a mobile ritual structure such as the yurt may actually resonate with other somewhat confusing aspects of ancient Chinese cosmology we have discussed. On reflection it seems odd to find various cosmological terms and symbols that so often reflect "insider knowledge" in the Dogon tradition openly expressed in various Chinese myths. It is as if some urgent imperative led the ancient Asian priests to adapt their entire system of cosmology, including the form of the aligned ritual structure, in ways that would best enable it to survive the difficulties of an uncertain future.

15

THE MAGIC SQUARE
AND THE NUMBERS
EIGHT AND NINE

Integral to both the plan of the ancient Chinese city and the nine-plot layout of the well-field system—and to concepts of divination in ancient China—is the notion of the Lo Shu square, or magic square, sometimes referred to as the "nine halls diagram." This figure is essentially a grid of nine squares, arranged like the well-field plots into a larger square, consisting of three squares per side (figure 15.1). Each smaller square is associated with one of the cardinal numbers from one to nine, arranged

4	9	2
3	5	7
8	1	6

Figure 15.1. The Lo Shu square, or magic square, sometimes referred to as the "nine halls diagram"

in such a way so that the sum of the three integers along any column or diagonal produces a total of fifteen.

Although there are variations in the myths, the invention of the magic square in China is traditionally assigned to Fu-xi at around 3000 BCE. According to one myth, Fu-xi (who, as we may recall, is sometimes referred to as Pau-xi) saw a tortoise climbing out of a river, called Lo Shu, and observed that the pattern of lines on the tortoise's back created a square grid, which he ultimately adopted as the basis for the magic square. There are a number of different ways in which integers may be assigned to the internal squares of the grid, each of which ultimately constitutes either a rotation or mirrored reflection of the square shown in figure 15.1. These figures are said to have provided Fu-xi with the inspiration to invent the eight trigrams, which later grew into the series of sixty-four hexagrams used in the process of divination in relation to the *Yijing*.[1]

The persistence of the figures of the square and the circle in Chinese cosmology in conjunction with the numbers eight and nine suggest that we may again want to explore these concepts as they are defined in our related cosmologies. For example, we know that in terms of ancient Chinese numerology, eight was the number associated with the concept of yin, while nine represented yang, and so from this perspective, the numbers seem to be intimately related to the primordial oppositions that define our cosmology. Likewise, these same symbolic assignments suggest that the concepts of yin and yang must be conceptually related to the process of squaring a circle.[2]

When we turn to the Egyptian hieroglyphic dictionary, we see that the Egyptian word for the number eight, *khemen,* is spelled with a circular glyph ⊜ that we said bears an outward similarity to the trigram diagrams of the *Yijing*.[3] As previously discussed, we know that in the Chinese tradition, the circle is a figure that is associated with the measures of the heavens. The Egyptian word for "nine," *petsch,* is spelled with the square glyph ☐, which in Chinese cosmology is associated with the measures of the Earth.[4]

Budge explains in his dictionary entry for the word *petsch-t*,* which he gives as the name of a very ancient god, that "it is probable that the true reading is *Pauti*."[5] We have said that we consider the Egyptian word *pau* to be a correlate to the Dogon *po*, which designates a primary atom-like component of matter. Meanwhile, Budge defines the Egyptian word *pau-t* to refer to the "stuff, matter, or material of which anything is made."[6] We have argued in prior volumes of this series that, in Dogon cosmology, the concept of mass or matter is symbolized by the term *earth*. So, from a symbolic standpoint, we could reasonably interpret the Egyptian word for "eight" to be given in terms of a Chinese symbol for the heavens, a concept that is sometimes referred to in our cosmologies symbolically as sky, and the Egyptian word for "nine" to be given in relation to a Chinese symbol for earth, a keyword in our cosmology for mass or matter.

It is clear that the numbers eight and nine could also well be interpreted within the context of the important cosmological concept of the squaring of a circle. The ancient Egyptians understood that, from a mathematical standpoint, the circumference of a circle with a diameter of nine units represents a very close approximation for the area of a square defined with eight of the same units per side. From this mathematical perspective, the numbers eight and nine come to be intimately related to the notion of squaring a circle. Furthermore the Egyptian number nine, which, based on Budge's explanatory note, we could reasonably associate with the phonetic root *pau*, is the number that the myth of the founding of the magic square associates symbolically with a Chinese deity who is sometimes called Pau-xi. In this way, the name of the deity gives sense to the very mythical action with which he is credited. Likewise, Pau-xi is the deity who is depicted as holding the square measure of the Earth, while Nu-wa is pictured holding a compass

---

*The spelling I used previously, in chapter 3, was *pestch-ti*, referring to nine gods. Here I use the spelling *petsch-t*. Egyptian spelling was not standardized, and a change in a single glyph can change the symbolic implication of a word entry. Budge gives both entries, and in each case I've used the one that relates to the specific point I'm making.

that she uses to measure the heavens. So the imagery of the icons that is assigned to these earliest Chinese deities can also be seen to uphold each aspect of the nine/eight, earth/sky, and squaring-of-circle symbolisms of the cosmology. We might even go so far as to say that the male/female pairing of the deities themselves, in the context of their defined mythical roles, could be seen as representative of the notion of squaring a circle.

To make matters even more interesting, there is an important Dogon myth in which a character named Ogo attempts to emulate the god Amma's creation of matter by breaking off a square piece of Amma's placenta. Budge tells us that the likely misreading of the Egyptian word for "nine" came out of the confusion between two similar written signs: *pestch* ⊖ and *paut* ⊙. The paut glyph, which Budge deems to constitute the proper spelling of the word, consists of a square that is set inside—or perhaps cut out of—a larger circle. This image, which seems to run parallel to the Dogon myth of Ogo, provides us with an additional rationale for the specific form taken by the Egyptian word for "nine." The image is suggestive both of Ogo's mythical act as it is described within Dogon mythology and of the cosmological notion of the squaring of a circle.

Some sources assert that the name of the river Lo Shu, from which Fu-xi's tortoise is said to have emerged, means "scroll of the river Lo." A scroll is a traditional surface for writing that, by its very form, reconciles the circular aspects of its rolled medium with the squared text that has been written on it. As such, we can think of it as also, in its own way, symbolizing the squaring of a circle. Synchronistic of the Chinese meaning, Budge's definition of the Egyptian word *shu* refers to "uninscribed rolls of papyri."[7] Likewise, the square markings on the underside of a tortoise shell such as the one observed by Fu-xi would seem to offer a kind of natural symbolism for the concept of squaring a circle. But the ostensibly misread Egyptian word *petsch* that Budge gives for "nine" is also a homonym for a term that Budge defines to mean "back, backbone, vertebrae."[8] These definitions call to mind the media on which the ancient Chinese oracle bone writings were traditionally inscribed. So, as with a scroll, we can say that the very choice of media for the oracle bone texts could also be said to reinforce the same "nine" symbolism that suggests the squaring of a circle.

We mentioned in chapter 10 that the word *khem/khemen,* which expresses the Egyptian number eight, was also an ancient name for the land of Egypt itself. The eight elemental deities of Egypt were referred to collectively as the Khemenu.[9] So in this way, we could say that the cosmological concept of the number eight seems to have been significant to ancient Egypt in much the same way that the symbolism of the number four was to ancient China.

With the way in which symbolism is defined in China and within our broader plan of cosmology, we can see that our explorations of the notions of squaring a circle and of reconciling the measures of the heavens with the measures of the Earth bring us back ultimately to a signature theme of the cosmological plan itself—the idea that what happens "above" is in some way fundamentally similar to what happens "below." The subtle implication is that it is humanity's task to reconcile the two. Metaphor after symbolic metaphor within the creation tradition, as we come to understand it more fully, seem to bring us back to this same tentative conclusion. So we are presented with the stupa as a grand mnemonic for the cosmology, whose geometry symbolizes earth and sky and whose plan illustrates the concept of the squaring of a circle. We see the legs of a turtle, whose very shape symbolizes the squaring of a circle, used as pillars to prop up the sky and thereby separate earth from sky. We see the primordial deities of Chinese cosmology assigned tools that are intimately related to a square and a circle and that are overtly used to measure heaven and Earth, or earth and sky. There is a consistent thread to this symbolism that, to our way of thinking, may constitute one of the fundamental messages of the ancient creation tradition itself.

16

RECONCILING CHINA WITH THE PLAN OF ANCIENT COSMOLOGY

In the preceding chapters we have discussed a fairly wide range of topics that relate to the creation traditions of ancient China and have outlined many ongoing correlations to the familiar system of cosmology that we have pursued in the previous volumes of this series. We came into these discussions believing that the ancient traditions of China would likely exhibit parallels to this system of cosmology, in part because of the success we had conducting our comparisons of the system to the cosmology and language of the Na-khi in *The Cosmological Origins of Myth and Symbol*. We knew that the Na-khi language, which is traditionally considered to be cosmology based, is thought to have influenced the development of written language in China, and we were also aware of a number of outward similarities between various individual Chinese and Egyptian glyphs. Likewise, we knew that the time frame of Chinese cosmology and civic development is understood to have been roughly contemporaneous with that of ancient Egypt and that the oldest myths in China are thought to have originated soon after the earliest myths of ancient Egypt. So, from several different perspectives, indications were that we would likely find consistencies with our cosmology in the ancient Chinese traditions.

However, we also knew coming into this study that the evidence on which comparisons to our cosmology would be based is relatively limited in China and that much of the documentation of this system did not come about until many centuries after the events themselves transpired. Perhaps in part because of this, there often tends to be little consensus among researchers of ancient Chinese traditions as to how to interpret this evidence, as compared with what exists among traditional Egyptologists or African anthropologists. So, from the very outset, it seemed uncertain whether we would ultimately find coherent answers to the often-difficult questions of Chinese cosmology.

It now remains for us to put our previous discussion into context, to essentially reconcile the comparisons we have made between individual elements of the Chinese creation traditions and our larger plan of cosmology. In the absence of that, all we would really have done is set down a series of stand-alone observations. We need to show on what reasonable basis the evidence from ancient China reflects the same kind of systemized plan of cosmology that we believe we have demonstrated in previous books for Africa, Egypt, India, and Tibet. In order to do this, we now need to take a step back from the material and reconsider the significant aspects of Chinese cosmology in overview.

First, we have shown that the creation themes of ancient Chinese tradition begin at the same starting points as are found in our plan of cosmology. Our discussion has demonstrated that, in the ancient Chinese view, creation emerges from the same kind of primordial chaos or disorder that is typically described in the other cosmologies we have studied and that this chaos is assigned many of the same familiar attributes. It is understood that this chaos is thought to precede the existence of time, to predate the formation of the universe, and to serve as a foundation for the processes that evoke matter. In regard to the formation of matter, this undifferentiated chaos is considered to be like water and is understood to be the primordial source of all material things. In accordance with what our cosmological plan would lead us to expect, the forms that emerge from this water-like chaos do so as a consequence of primordial vibrations and make their appearance through what is compared to a phase transition—a process similar to that of ice turning into water, water becoming water vapor, or gelatin gelling. In regard to the formation of the universe, this initial state of chaos is thought to have resided inside a cosmogonic egg, similar to what is described in the Dogon tradition as Amma's egg. The egg eventually ruptures, and the unrealized potential that resides within the egg bursts out to create the universe as we know it.

Next, we find that Chinese cosmology is traditionally understood in terms of the same parallel themes of our cosmological plan. Symbols that, on one hand, are described in relation to the formation of the universe and of matter are also alternately interpreted in the context of biological reproduction. The parallel nature of these themes is evident in traditional descriptions of the stages of Daoism, and we see evidence of this dual symbolism in Chinese and Japanese terms that are used to describe the plan of an ancient Chinese city. To the extent that this plan corresponds to the ground plan of an aligned ritual structure like a Buddhist stupa, we see symbolism that is interpreted to reflect concepts of both cosmological and biological creation. For example, the axes that divide the city into four quadrants are understood to align it cosmologically with the universe, while the city's progressive divisions call to mind the divisions of a fertilized egg. Likewise, this parallelism has also been evident in individual Chinese cosmological words and symbols, which are frequently defined in terms of both themes. Similarly, our comparisons of other cultures' languages to ancient Egyptian words consistently point to references that relate to both cosmological and biological themes.

As is true for our plan of cosmology, the processes of creation in China rest on a principle of paired opposites. This is a principle that originates in China with the concepts of yin and yang and is graphically illustrated in the Chinese yin/yang symbol. Chinese cosmology gives expression to this principle in many of the same ways as it is given in our cosmological plan. This symbolism starts with emphasis on the notion of male versus female, as is illustrated from earliest times in China with the pairing of the primordial creator-deities Nu-wa and Fu-xi. Likewise, this same principle is given in mythological descriptions, with such classic examples as the opposition of darkness and light, or through mythic descriptions of the separation of earth and sky. It is also exemplified in China—again as in our plan of cosmology—in terms of the counterposed states of classic primordial elements such as water, fire, wind, and earth.

We have seen that the evolution of matter in ancient China is configured in conceptual worlds or levels of creation, comparable to the three worlds of matter as they are described in the Dogon tradition. As is true for the Dogon, the references of ancient Chinese cosmology convey a clear sense that the processes by which matter is created are conceptualized as ascending upward through these worlds, with the idea that significant transformations occur in the form of things as they pass through these stages and between worlds. Our discussion shows that both the seven stages of creation in Daoism and the eight trigrams of the *Yijing* relate symbolically to these processes of transformation. We can relate the Chinese symbolism to descriptions of the Dogon Second World, where matter in its original wavelike form has been disrupted and is said to be transformed and effectively reordered.

The notion that the stages of creation ascend upward was also conveyed in ancient China through the same symbolic metaphor of a world tree that we find present in our other cosmologies. Furthermore, there are additional Chinese references to a symbolic mulberry tree (a term that is mentioned and has significance in the Dogon tradition) associated with the upward ascension of matter that holds a place comparable to the tree of life, familiarly associated with the growth of space in our cosmological plan. The parallel nature of the symbolism associated with these two mythical trees reflects the ongoing correlations that are made within our cosmologies between the processes of the microcosm and those of the macrocosm. Both uphold the same fundamental principle of the cosmological plan that is embodied by the notion of a mother goddess and that is expressed in the signature phrase "as above, so below."

There were associations in ancient China between the lower worlds of creation and concepts of death. These are comparable to the many associations we find in ancient Egypt between the mythical underworld and concepts and rituals of death. Such associations become more evident when we examine Chinese terms whose meanings pertain to wrapped cloth and to the ritual wrapping of a body, references that call to mind the ritualized wrapping of an Egyptian mummy. We see similar associations with death and transformation in Chinese symbolism that relates to the mythical notion of the turtle, expressed in the ancient Chinese belief that the spirit of a dead person conceptually sheds its body as if it were clothing. It is this same symbolism that we see expressed in Egyptian descriptions of the journey a dead person's soul makes through the mythical Tuat, or Duat.

Like the base plan of a Dogon granary or a Buddhist stupa, concepts of space as they were applied at all levels of land management in ancient China began with a profane space that was made sacred by ritually differentiating it from the surrounding disorder or chaos. The ritual processes that are inherent both in the Chinese concept of space and in that of a Buddhist stupa rest on the belief that the specific method employed to align the space replicates the processes by which multiplicity emerges from unity. In both cases, the area defined by this alignment process is then segmented into four quadrants by two axes, the orientations of which are established through a matching series of geometric measurements. This geometry's ultimate purpose is to orient the space locally to the four cardinal points and cosmically to the larger universe. This same concept of sacred space is alternately expressed in both the Dogon and Chinese traditions in terms of four squared plots of land, set in the shape of a cross—a configuration whose shape ultimately defines nine square plots. We see this conveyed both through the details of the well-field plan, a system that seemingly constitutes the fundamental unit of land division in both Dogon and Chinese agriculture, and through the cosmologically inspired plan of the ancient Chinese city. Comparable symbolism would appear to be reflected in—and provide a sensible symbolic rationale for—the shape and traditional meaning of the Egyptian town glyph ⊗.

We learn through examples given in Chinese cosmology that the square and the circle are taken in an early mythical context as symbols of earth and space, respectively. By that same logic, the cosmological concept of the squaring of a circle, which is at the heart of the Chinese concept of land management, can be understood to reconcile the measures of the heavens with measures of the Earth. This would again seem to be in accordance with the defining theme of our cosmology: "as above, so below." These concepts of square and round geometry are explicitly assigned to the Chinese creator-deities Nu-wa and Fu-xi by way of the tools of measurement they are traditionally depicted as holding (an architect's square and a compass) and provide a tangible link between the ancient Chinese myths of creation and the overall scheme of ancient Chinese land management.

We also see examples in the ancient Chinese creation tradition of many of the familiar constructs of our cosmological plan. These begin with the notion of the unformed universe conceptualized in the shape of two cones, comparable to Amma's egg in the Dogon tradition, and of two facing thorns that, for the Dogon, preceded the formation of the universe. We find a pool of water used in the Chinese tradition to symbolize the source of creation in relation to the mulberry tree. We find the image of a raised tent given, again as with the Dogon, to help visualize the initial transformations of matter in the seven stages of Daoism. We see a matching cosmological construct in the ancient Chinese conception of the sun, symbolized by the archetypical figure of a circle that surrounds a central dot. Moreover, we also find important symbolic aspects of the matching Dogon egg-in-a-ball construct associated with this Chinese sun symbol. Perhaps most significantly, not only do we find the concept of an aligned ritual structure itself in ancient China, we also see many of the expected symbolic attributes of a Buddhist stupa traditionally associated with aligned structures in China.

We see resemblances to our cosmological plan in civic practices of ancient China that are comparable to those found in ancient Egypt. These include such conventions as the observance of a 360-day calendar based on a ten-day week and the development of a hieroglyphic language that seems to have adopted aspects of cosmological symbology. These resemblances also include the use of the cubit as a traditional unit of measurement, which we consider to be a signature of our plan of cosmology. We see resemblances to ancient Egypt in the earliest Chinese civic centers, which are deemed to have grown up around ritual sites and, according to Paul Wheatley and Walter Fairservis, are thought to have functioned similarly to their Egyptian counterparts. Looked at from the perspective of civic practices, we again see correlations to the Dogon in the concept of the well-field system, which seems to represent—at the very least—the earliest theoretic construct of agriculture in ancient China.

Many of the mythological traditions of ancient China also uphold expectations we may hold based on knowledge of our cosmological plan. For example, we find that venerated mythic Chinese ancestors who are closely associated with the introduction of civilizing skills play a central role in the ancient Chinese tradition. As is true in ancient Egypt and for the Na-khi, we find an extensive list of ancient Chinese kings or emperors who are interpreted by modern-day scholars as being quasi-mythical and quasi-historical in nature, but who bear demonstrable relationships to our cosmology. We find that the notion of a deity in China originated with myths relating to a great mother goddess similar to the Egyptian goddess Neith and who is associated with a Chinese creator-god who could be comparable to Amen or Atum in Egypt or to Amma among the Dogon. We learn that, as in Egypt and for the Dogon and the Na-khi, there was a mythic tradition in China in which humanity was said to have been created by these deities from clay.

We see many of the cosmological metaphors that are evident in our plan of cosmology also at play in the ancient Chinese tradition. These begin with archetypical primordial elements that are symbolized by water, fire, wind, and earth, but in China they seem to have been extended beyond the four classic Greek elements to include elements such as wood and metal, perhaps to facilitate correlation to the eight stages of creation represented by the trigrams of the *Yijing*. Alternately, perhaps the additional Chinese elements represent the same opposing attributes of these primordial elements as are expressed in our cosmological plan. These are given in the cosmology as the notions of earth versus sky, wind as compared with still air, fire versus wood, and liquid water or wetness as compared with the concept of dryness. Like the cubit, we also consider these four-stage metaphors to represent a signature aspect of our ancient plan of cosmology.

Evidence of one such metaphor is found in China, given in terms of conceptual categories of animals that, in the Dogon tradition, begin with insects and end with birds. Our comparison of the oracle bone fish glyph and the Dogon nummo fish drawing serves to associate the Chinese glyph with this metaphoric sequence of symbols. Within our broader plan of cosmology, the progression symbolized by the fish culminates with the emergence of mass or matter, which is symbolized by the shape of a hemisphere. In China, we find that the four-legged turtle, with its hemispheric shell, seemingly corresponds to this same stage of matter.

Within the plan of cosmology, these metaphors work on one level to help us categorize a complex set of cosmological symbols and organize them in their proper sequence. As in the Dogon tradition, Chinese cosmology was understood to represent a kind of world plan by which initiates could organize important aspects of daily life. The aligned granary structure of the Dogon encompassed an entire system of zoology that was used to categorize all of the various families and classes of animals. This zoology provided a progression of creatures whose natural groupings and interrelationships were tagged metaphorically to the progressive stages of cosmological and biological creation. Through this process, each class of animals came to symbolize a specific stage or concept of creation. We see these same staged concepts reflected in the animal symbolism that defines various deities in Egyptian art and in the concepts that are reflected symbolically in the written names for each animal.

In China, we see evidence of similar creation symbolism associated with classes of animals expressed both in myth and, most overtly, through the later construct of the zodiac. As was suggested by Marcel Griaule during his discussions of Dogon cosmology, we see that the zodiac system combines a number of the physical, conceptual, and symbolic elements that we associate with the aligned Buddhist stupa or the Dogon granary structure. Animal symbolism is expressed in the Chinese tradition both in terms of overt attributes of various animals such as the turtle and the serpent and in terms of animal names that, as in ancient Egypt, appear to reflect root cosmological terms. Likewise, as in Dogon and Egyptian myths, animals are seen to play pivotal roles in various Chinese myths, for example, in the role played by the birds in the myth of the mulberry tree and in the story of Nu-wa, who appropriates the legs of a tortoise to serve as pillars to support the sky.

A number of other examples of matched symbolic images and descriptions seem to tie the Chinese creation tradition to our plan of cosmology. We find this in the image of thorns as it is used to represent the unformed universe. It is apparent in the characterization of the primordial source of creation as a pool of water. It is found in the image of matter drawing upward like a tent and in the notion of pivoting that is used to describe the complex movement that is associated with the first vibrations of matter. It is evident in the description of a Second World of creation that is conceptualized in terms of the rays of a star. It is found in the common numerology and cardinal counting through which various concepts of creation are expressed. We can see this in the use of the symbol of the drum to convey the concept of vibration. We see it again in the common use of images of eggs and wombs to symbolize concepts of cosmological and biological creation, respectively. We see obvious matching examples in the specific ways that symbolism is assigned to various animals based on their attributes.

Perhaps the most pervasive and compelling parallels between the ancient Chinese creation tradition and our ancient cosmological plan are found in the specific terms and phonetic values that define their elements. We have seen these connections demonstrated throughout our discussion in the previous chapters, where they seem to shed new light on various poorly understood aspects of ancient Chinese cosmology. In some cases, the Chinese term is expressed using phonetic values that are already familiar to us, and so points the way to a likely correlation. In others, the link to our cosmology is made through the multiple meanings that are assigned to the Chinese term. In either case, the usages appear to cross the boundaries of culture and language, and so the dictionaries of other cultures become an unexpected but effective tool for understanding the Chinese references. In our opinion, the ease and consistency with which we are able to demonstrate the commonality of these terms upholds our belief that the matching sets of terms came from a common original source.

One very telling outward expression of this commonality of cosmological terms between cultures is illustrated in the apparent naming conventions we see reflected in the names of ancient tribal cultures from various regions, including China. One of these conventions, which we again take as a signature of the cosmology, identifies the tribe in terms of a specific stage of creation that may have been emphasized by the tribe, as is signaled by the form of the ancient Chinese name Fu-xi. We can also hardly overstate the significance of the commonality of form in which the ancient Egyptian and Chinese words for "week" were expressed. The glyphs of this simple word eloquently demonstrate how the self-same principles of cosmology seem to underlie the earliest written expression in both China and Egypt.

In China—again, as we would expect based on knowledge of the other ancient cosmologies we have studied—important conceptual terms tend to take the form of compound words and are often composed of phonetic values that carry specific symbolism. We see this convention perhaps most vividly demonstrated in the Chinese word *Yijing*, but we have noted its expression in a wide variety of names and terms of ancient Chinese cosmology. We have seen that coherent definitions of many of these root phonetic values are to be found in Genevieve Calame-Griaule's *Dictionnaire Dogon* and in Budge's *An Egyptian Hieroglyphic Dictionary*. During our studies of Egyptian hieroglyphic words in *Sacred Symbols of the Dogon*, we discussed many of these phonetic values as they relate to the pronunciation of individual Egyptian glyphs and the concepts those glyphs are thought to represent. We observed a high degree of predictability between the phonetic values themselves and specific cosmological concepts represented by the words. Many of those same phonetic values and concept pairings seemed to be upheld by pronunciations among the Dogon, where, from the standpoint of cosmology, words are only spoken, not written. We concluded that there might have been a systematized relationship in ancient times between certain phonetic values and well-defined cosmological concepts. A similar relationship appears to be upheld in the various Chinese terms we have examined.

In sum, we find a broad range of traditional aspects of ancient Chinese cosmology that conform well to the contours of our ancient plan of cosmology. The parallels we have discussed touch on virtually every significant aspect of the cosmology and its associated civilizing plan. These parallels express themselves through the themes and characters of ancient Chinese mythology, through the beliefs that underlie the most ancient concepts of creation in China and in the imagery through which these concepts are given expression. We find ongoing commonality in the terms used to describe ancient Chinese cosmology and our cosmology. The Chinese terms are expressed using the same conventions of symbolism as in our civilizing plan and are often characterized by the same phonetic and representational forms. These cosmological terms are associated with the same sets of matched but logically distant definitions that we have long taken to be a signature of our ancient plan of cosmology.

Likewise, we find evidence of this cosmology in virtually every aspect of ancient Chinese life. We recognize it in the descriptions of the earliest Chinese deities, in their relationships to concepts of creation, and in the acts they are said to have performed. Such evidence takes its expression in the earliest traditions of ancestor worship in ancient China and in the civilizing skills with which they are associated. We find it in the most fundamental ancient unit of measure in China—the cubit—and in the fundamental units of ancient land division in China. We find it in the theoretic well-field plan of ancient Chinese agriculture. We see it in the traditional architectural layout of an ancient Chinese city. We find this evidence in the very processes by which an ancient Chinese city was aligned to its surroundings. We see it in the base plan and extended symbolism of various ancient Chinese aligned ritual shrines. We find it in ancient Chinese concepts of time and in the formulation of the calendars the Chinese used to measure out the year. We find it in the symbolic implementation of the earliest Chinese hieroglyphic writings.

Our plan of cosmology reveals itself in many of the traditional philosophical constructs that arose in ancient China. This philosophy begins with the notion of yin and yang, extends to the philosophical underpinnings of the *Yijing,* and is arguably enshrined in the very concept of the mandala. Our cosmology is inherent in the ancient Chinese concept of the magic square. Later in history, many important symbolic constructs of our cosmological plan come together in the form of the Chinese zodiac.

The ancient Chinese creation tradition is often associated with what might be described as a more mobile form of our familiar cosmological plan. We notice that many Chinese references that typically constitute "insider knowledge" in other cosmologies often seem to be given in an outwardly accessible but disguised form, carried forward as details highlighted in the myths of ancient Chinese culture. This important cosmological information seems to have been unknowingly carried forward in public by noninitiates to the esoteric tradition through stories that are contextualized as quasi-mythic histories of popular ancient emperors. This information is hidden within the constructs of the trigrams of the *Yijing,* in the mythic stages of creation that typify Daoism, and in the animal groups that compose the Chinese zodiac. As in other cultures, we find useful information couched in the very terms of ancient Chinese cosmology. It also seems to have been carried forward, down through the generations, in the Mongolian yurt, a structure that again takes the form of a kind of mobile ritual shrine similar to the stupa.

This recurring trend toward mobility suggests that life in some parts of ancient China may never have taken on the kind of lasting stability that characterized much of the history of ancient Egypt or that we see preserved culturally by the priestly Dogon tribe or in the writings of the Tibetan Na-khi. This feature of the Chinese myths calls to mind the story of the Exodus from Egypt and the traditional Passover Seder, where, in both cases, we encounter an unexpectedly coherent series of cosmological symbols and themes that may also have been alternately encoded, perhaps as a kind of mobile mythic history. This again occurred at a time in Egyptian history when great instability is thought to have arisen, so it might be seen to have been a hedge against outright loss of an esoteric tradition that, in other cultures, seemed rooted in the unstated expectation of long-standing societal stability.

Perhaps as a final conclusion to this study, given the many diverse facets of the Chinese creation tradition that lend themselves to favorable comparison with our theorized plan of ancient cosmology, it seems fair to say that the ancient Chinese creation tradition presents a very close match for that plan as we have come to understand it through our studies of other cultures. Not only do the traditional viewpoints we cite about ancient Chinese cosmology seem to uphold the key elements of that plan, they also provide us with significant new rationales by which to clarify some of the less well-understood elements of that plan. Furthermore, just as we found during our exploration of the practices and language of the Tibetan Na-khi, the plan once again shows itself to be a reliable predictor of what can ultimately be shown to be true regarding myth and symbol in the earliest days of ancient Chinese culture. Based on its ability to successfully do this, we can say that the plan easily passes what is perhaps the most essential test of a reasonable scientific theory.

NOTES

INTRODUCTION

1. Allan, *Shape of the Turtle,* 20.
2. Ibid., 24.
3. Girardot, *Myth and Meaning,* 21.

CHAPTER 1. CONTOURS OF A SHARED CREATION TRADITION

1. Budge, *Egyptian Hieroglyphic Dictionary,* 53–54.

CHAPTER 2. EARLY CHINESE CONCEPTS OF COSMOLOGY

1. Lewis, *Construction of Space,* 1–2.
2. Bruya, "Chaos as the Inchoate."
3. Lewis, *Construction of Space,* 2.
4. Snodgrass, *Symbolism of the Stupa,* 21–22.
5. Budge, *Egyptian Hieroglyphic Dictionary,* 102a.
6. Lewis, *Construction of Space,* 1–2.
7. Pregadio, *Routledge Encyclopedia of Taoism,* 973–74.
8. Girardot, *Myth and Meaning,* 19–20.
9. Scranton, *Cosmological Origins,* 98.
10. Morrison, *Dictionary of the Chinese Language,* 15.
11. Berriman, *Historical Metrology,* 71.
12. Lewis, *Construction of Space,* 247.

13. Wheatley, *Pivot of the Four Quarters,* 418.

14. "Ancient Chinese Cosmology," Hollow Earth, August 22, 2011, http://hollowplanet.blogspot.com/2011/08/ancient-chinese-cosmology.html.

15. Meyer, *China: A Concise History,* 118. For more information, see Tom Retter, "China's Dynasties: Prehistory and the Xia," Book from the Sky, April 23, 2012, http://bookfromthesky.net/2012/04/23/chinas-dynasties-the-xia.

16. Wheatley, *Pivot of the Four Quarters,* 477.

17. Smith, *Fathoming the Cosmos,* 220.

CHAPTER 3. ANCESTOR-TEACHERS
IN THE CHINESE COSMOLOGY

1. Allan, *Shape of the Turtle,* 50–51.

2. Theobald Ulrich, "Chinese History—Shang Dynasty 商 (17th to 11th cent. BC): Science, Technology, and Inventions," ChinaKnowledge: A Universal Guide for China Studies, www.chinaknowledge.de/History/Myth/shang-tech.html (accessed February 5, 2014).

3. Wheatley, *Pivot of the Four Quarters,* 11.

4. Budge, *Egyptian Hieroglyphic Dictionary,* 896a.

5. Ibid., 22–23.

6. Xiaoping, *Worshiping the Three Sage Kings,* 7.

7. "Fu-Xi," Cultural China, http://history.cultural-china.com/en/46H5031H11121.html (accessed February 10, 2014).

8. Budge, *Egyptian Hieroglyphic Dictionary,* 689b.

9. Ibid., 134a.

10. Ibid., 41a.

11. Xiaoping, *Worshiping the Three Sage Kings,* 20.

12. Fong et al. *Chinese America,* 64.

13. Budge, *Egyptian Hieroglyphic Dictionary,* 11b.

14. Ibid.

15. Ibid., 231a–34a.

16. Allan, *Shape of the Turtle,* 65.

17. Xiaoping, *Worshiping the Three Sage Kings,* 26.

18. Ibid., 34–43.

19. Budge, *Egyptian Hieroglyphic Dictionary,* 144–57.

20. Ibid., 331–32.

21. Ibid., 249–51.

22. Xiaoping, *Worshiping the Three Sage Kings,* 44–53.

23. Budge, *Egyptian Hieroglyphic Dictionary,* 720–29.

24. Girardot, *Myth and Meaning,* 99–100.

25. Ibid., 141.

CHAPTER 4.
THE CHINESE CONCEPT OF THE MULBERRY TREE

1. Snodgrass, *Symbolism of the Stupa,* 166.

2. Allan, *Shape of the Turtle,* 27.

3. Budge, *Egyptian Hieroglyphic Dictionary,* 27b.

4. Snodgrass, *Symbolism of the Stupa,* 166–67.

5. Calame-Griaule, *Dictionnaire Dogon,* 242.

CHAPTER 5.
THE WELL-FIELD SYSTEM

1. Griaule, *Conversations with Ogotemmeli,* 88.

2. Griaule, "Dogon of the French Sudan," 94–95.

3. Griaule, *Conversations with Ogotemmeli,* 88.

4. Ibid., 76.

5. Budge, *Egyptian Hieroglyphic Dictionary,* 120–21.

6. Ibid., 490ab.

7. Ingrid Salomon, "Surveying in Ancient Egypt," School of Surveying and Spatial Information Systems, University of New South Wales, www.gmat .unsw.edu.au/currentstudents/ug/projects/salmon/salmon.htm (accessed February 5, 2014).

8. Budge, *Egyptian Hieroglyphic Dictionary,* 43b.

9. Hsu, *Ancient China in Transition,* 196.

10. Wheatley, *Pivot of the Four Quarters,* 132–34.

11. Rosemont, *Explorations in Early Chinese Cosmology,* 141.

12. Ibid., 133–34, 141.

13. Snodgrass, *Architecture, Time, and Eternity,* 343–45.

CHAPTER 6.
THE EARLIEST CHINESE CITIES

1. Wheatley, *Pivot of the Four Quarters,* 231.

2. Yanxin, Cai. "Chinese Ancient Cities: The Grid System, Feng Shui, and

Il Fong," Lands of Wisdom, http://landsofwisdom.com/?p=3491 (accessed February 5, 2014).

3. Wheatley, *Pivot of the Four Quarters,* 423–25.

4. Ibid., 426.

5. Scranton, *Cosmological Origins,* 113.

6. Wheatley, *Pivot of the Four Quarters,* 427.

7. Ibid.

8. Ibid., 414.

9. Coleridge, letter to Sara Hutchinson. The reference is to Browne's *The Garden of Cyrus; or, The Quincunciall, Lozenge, or Network Plantations of the Ancients, Artificially, Naturally, Mystically Considered.*

10. Wheatley, *Pivot of the Four Quarters,* 414.

11. Ibid., 231.

12. Ibid., 428.

13. "Architecture—Asia—Chinese Temples and Residences," Science Encyclopedia, http://science.jrank.org/pages/8359/Architecture-Asia-Chinese-Temples-Residences.html (accessed February 5, 2014).

14. Snodgrass, *Architecture, Time, and Eternity,* 331–33.

15. Budge, *Egyptian Hieroglyphic Dictionary,* cxxvi–cxxvii.

16. Ibid., 41b.

17. David W. Pankenier, "Cosmic Capitals and Numinous Precincts in Early China," Cosmology, www.journalofcosmology.com/AncientAstronomy100.html (accessed February 10, 2014).

CHAPTER 7. DAOISM AND THE SEVEN STAGES OF CREATION

1. Budge, *Egyptian Hieroglyphic Dictionary,* cxxvi.

2. Ibid., 144b.

3. Girardot, *Myth and Meaning,* 119–21.

4. Budge, *Egyptian Hieroglyphic Dictionary,* 153b.

5. Ibid., 131b.

6. Ibid., 536a.

7. Ibid., 224b.

8. Calame-Griaule, *Dictionnaire Dogon,* 156.

9. Ibid., 265.

10. Budge, *Egyptian Hieroglyphic Dictionary,* 820b.

11. Ibid., 815a.

12. Ibid., cxxv.

13. Ibid., 299a.

14. Ibid., 296b.

15. Calame-Griaule, *Dictionnaire Dogon,* 182.

16. Budge, *Egyptian Hieroglyphic Dictionary,* 269a.

17. Ibid., 837–38.

18. Ibid., 683a.

19. Calame-Griaule, *Dictionnaire Dogon,* 240.

20. Ibid., 285–86.

21. Budge, *Egyptian Hieroglyphic Dictionary,* 833–36.

22. Girardot, *Myth and Meaning,* 45.

CHAPTER 8. THE MANDALA

1. Jung, *Mandala Symbolism,* 3.

2. Snodgrass, *Symbolism of the Stupa,* 104.

3. Jung, *Mandala Symbolism,* 4.

4. Patrick A. George, "Mandala: Buddhist Tantric Designs," Scaffold: WWW Architectural Project, http://ccat.sas.upenn.edu/george/mandala.html (accessed February 10, 2014).

5. Ibid.

6. Lessing and Wayman, *Introduction to the Buddhist Tantric Systems,* 270, note 1.

7. Snodgrass, *Symbolism of the Stupa,* 104.

8. Ibid., 105.

9. Budge, *Egyptian Hieroglyphic Dictionary,* 269a.

10. Snodgrass, *Symbolism of the Stupa,* 105.

11. Budge, *Egyptian Hieroglyphic Dictionary,* 805a.

12. Lewis, *Construction of Space,* 154.

13. Budge, *Egyptian Hieroglyphic Dictionary,* 271b.

14. Snodgrass, *Architecture, Time, and Eternity,* 343–45.

15. Rosemont, *Explorations in Early Chinese Cosmology,* 154.

CHAPTER 9. THE YIJING (I CHING)

1. Smith, *Fathoming the Cosmos,* 3.

2. Ibid., 38.

3. Ibid., 8–9.

4. Calame-Griaule, *Dictionnaire Dogon,* 115.

5. Budge, *Egyptian Hieroglyphic Dictionary,* 30a.

6. Ibid., cxlvi.

7. Ibid., 534b.

8. Ibid., cxlv.

9. Ibid., 526b.

10. Calame-Griaule, *Dictionnaire Dogon,* 138.

11. Scranton, *Sacred Symbols of the Dogon,* 136.

12. Ibid., 57.

13. Smith, *Fathoming the Cosmos,* 38.

14. Calame-Griaule, *Dictionnaire Dogon,* 34.

15. Budge, *Egyptian Hieroglyphic Dictionary,* 258a.

16. Ibid.

17. Ibid., 44a.

18. Ibid., 43b.

19. Calame-Griaule, *Dictionnaire Dogon,* 132.

CHAPTER 10. THE EIGHT TRIGRAMS

1. Smith, *Fathoming the Cosmos,* 29.

2. Calame-Griaule, *Dictionnaire Dogon,* 19.

3. Budge, *Egyptian Hieroglyphic Dictionary,* 230b.

4. Ibid., 843b.

5. Ibid., 536a.

6. Ibid., 673b.

7. Ibid.

8. Ibid., 824b.

9. Ibid., 643b.

10. Ibid., 589b.

11. Ibid., 665b.

12. Ibid., 745–46.

13. Ibid., 547b.

14. Ibid., 546a.

CHAPTER 11. THE ZODIAC

1. Robert Powell, "The Babylonian Zodiac," Astrogeographia, www
.astrogeographia.org/articles/BabylonianZodiac (accessed February 10, 2014).

2. Griaule, *Conversations with Ogotemmeli,* 209–16.

3. Snodgrass, *Symbolism of the Stupa,* 33.

4. Liddell and Scott, *Greek-English Lexicon,* s.v. "Perseus."

5. Budge, *Egyptian Hieroglyphic Dictionary,* 691a.

6. Ibid., 647a.

7. Ibid., 685b.

8. Ibid., 689b.

9. Ibid., 165a.

10. Ibid., 31b.

11. Ibid., 42b.

12. Ibid., 236b.

13. Ibid., 32a.

14. Ibid., 159b.

15. Ibid., 913a.

16. Ibid., 29.

17. Snodgrass, *Symbolism of the Stupa,* 185.

18. Budge, *Egyptian Hieroglyphic Dictionary,* 598ab.

19. Snodgrass, *Symbolism of the Stupa,* 45.

20. Budge, *Egyptian Hieroglyphic Dictionary,* 200a.

CHAPTER 12. THE COSMOLOGICAL ROLE OF THE TURTLE

1. Allan, *Shape of the Turtle,* 104.

2. Ibid., 1.

3. Dallapiccola, *Dictionary of Hindu Lore and Legend.*

4. Allan, *Shape of the Turtle,* 104.

5. Griaule and Dieterlen, *Pale Fox,* 221.

6. Budge, *Egyptian Hieroglyphic Dictionary,* 755–58.

7. Allan, *Shape of the Turtle,* 29.

8. Ibid., 105–7.

CHAPTER 13. ORACLE BONE WRITING

1. "Oracle Bone Script," Omniglot: The Online Encyclopedia of Writing Systems and Languages, www.omniglot.com/chinese/jiaguwen.htm (accessed February 10, 2014).

2. Ibid.

3. Max Dashú, "Wu: Female Shamans in Ancient China," Suppressed Histories Archives, 2011, www.suppressedhistories.net/articles2/WuFSAC.pdf (accessed February 10, 2014). There is also an excerpt and an online discussion at www.sourcememory.net/veleda/?p=104 (accessed February 10, 2014).

4. Xu, Pankenier, and Jiang, *East Asian Archeoastronomy,* 138.

5. Scranton, *Cosmological Origins,* 148–61.

6. Rock, *Na-Khi–English Encyclopedic Dictionary,* xix–xx.

CHAPTER 14.
SYMBOLISM OF THE *GER,*
OR YURT

1. "Yurt," New World Encyclopedia, www.newworldencyclopedia.org/entry/Yurt (accessed February 10, 2014).

2. "Encyclopedic Entry: Yurt," National Geographic Education, http://education.nationalgeographic.com/education/encyclopedia/yurt/?ar_a=1 (accessed February 10, 2014).

3. David Stronach, "On the Antiquity of the Yurt: Evidence from Arjan and Elsewhere," *The Silk Road,* vol. 2, no. 1 (2004), www.silkroadfoundation .org/newsletter/ 2004vol2num1/yurt.htm.

4. Jessica Crabtree, "NPR Commentary: Navajos in Tibet," Jessica Crabtree: Native American Portraits and Wildlife, www.jessicacrabtree.com/journal1/2011/09/npr-navajos-in-tibet (accessed February 10, 2014).

5. Gregory A. Little, "DNA Analysis on Native Americans," Biblioteca Pleyades, www.bibliotecapleyades.net/ciencia/ciencia_adn05.htm (accessed February 10, 2014). See section headed "Confirming the Siberian Migration."

6. "Mongolian Cosmology," Circle of Tengerism, www.tengerism.org/cosmology .html (accessed February 10, 2014).

CHAPTER 15. THE MAGIC SQUARE
AND THE NUMBERS EIGHT AND NINE

1. Jenny Kile, "The Lo Shu Magic Square Illustrates an Inspiring Formation," Suite, www.suite101.com/article/the-lo-shu-magic-square-illustrates-an -inspiring-formation-a382426 (accessed February 10, 2014). Reference also confirmed by Simona Gauri, "Chinese Divination: The Magic Square, the I

Ching, Trigrams, and Hexagrams," Lands of Wisdom, www.landsofwisdom
.com/?p=989 (accessed February 10, 2014).

2. Snodgrass, *Symbolism of the Stupa,* 244.

3. Budge, *Egyptian Hieroglyphic Dictionary,* 547b.

4. Ibid., 250a.

5. Ibid.

6. Ibid., 230b.

7. Ibid., 733a.

8. Ibid., 250a.

9. Ibid., 548a.

BIBLIOGRAPHY

Allan, Sarah. *The Shape of the Turtle: Myth, Art, and Cosmos in Early China.* Albany, N.Y.: State University of New York Press, 1991.

Berriman, Algernon Edward. *Historical Metrology: A New Analysis of the Archaeological and the Historical Evidence Relating to Weights and Measures.* Westport, Conn.: Greenwood Press, 1969.

Bruya, Brian J. "Chaos as the Inchoate: The Early Chinese Aesthetic of Spontaneity." In *Aesthetics and Chaos: Investigating a Creative Complicity,* edited by Grazia Marchianò, 115–135. Turin, Italy: Trauben Editions, 2002.

Budge, E. A. Wallis. *An Egyptian Hieroglyphic Dictionary.* New York: Dover Publications, Inc., 1978.

Calame-Griaule, Genevieve. *Dictionnaire Dogon.* Paris: Librarie C. Klincksieck, 1968.

Coleridge, Samuel Taylor. Letter to Sara Hutchinson, on two and one-half flyleaves of a volume containing Browne's *Vulgar Errors, Religio Medici, Hydriotaphia,* and *Garden of Cyrus* (London, 1658), now in the Berg Collection, New York Public Library. See *Coleridge on the Seventeenth Century,* edited by Roberta Florence Brinkley. Durham, N.C.: Duke University Press, 1955.

Dallapiccola, Anna Libera. *Dictionary of Hindu Lore and Legend.* New York: Thames and Hudson, 2002.

Eno, R. "The Economy of Early China: The Treatise on Food and Money." Indiana University online, www.indiana.edu/~g380/2.2-Food_and_Money-2010.pdf. Accessed February 5, 2014.

Fong, Colleen, Marlon K. Hom, Madeline Hsu, et al., eds. *Chinese America:*

History and Perspectives. San Francisco: Chinese Historical Society of America, 2003.

Girardot, Norman J. *Myth and Meaning in Early Daoism: The Theme of Chaos (Hundun).* Berkeley: University of California Press, 1988.

Griaule, Marcel. *Conversations with Ogotemmeli.* Oxford, England: Oxford University Press, 1970.

———. "The Dogon of the French Sudan." In *African Worlds: Studies in the Cosmological Ideas and Social Values of African Peoples,* edited by Daryll Forde, 83–110. Oxford, England: James Currey Publishers, 1999. First published by Oxford University Press for the International African Institute in 1954.

Griaule, Marcel, and Germaine Dieterlen. *The Pale Fox.* Paris: Continuum Foundation, 1986.

Hagan, Helene. *The Shining Ones: An Entymological Essay on the Amazigh Roots of Egyptian Civilization.* Bloomington, Ind.: Xlibris, 2000.

Hsu, Cho-yun. *Ancient China in Transition: An Analysis of Social Mobilization 722–222 B.C.* Stanford, Calif.: The Board of Trustees of Leland Stanford University, 1965.

Jung, Carl Gustav. *Mandala Symbolism.* Translated by R. F. C. Hull. Princeton, N.J.: Princeton University Press, 1972.

Kemery, Becky. "Life within the Ger: The Sacred Circle." Section head in *Yurts: Living in the Round.* Layton, Utah: Gibbs Smith, 2006.

Lessing, F. D., and Alex Wayman. *Introduction to the Buddhist Tantric Systems.* New Delhi, India: Motilal Banarsidass Publishers, 2008.

Lewis, Mark Edward. *The Construction of Space in Early China.* Albany, N.Y.: State University of New York Press, 2006.

Liddell, Henry George, and Robert Scott. *A Greek-English Lexicon.* Oxford, England: Oxford University Press, 1996.

Mathieu, Christine. *A History and Anthropological Study of the Ancient Kingdoms of the Sino-Tibetan Borderland—Naxi and Mosuo.* Lewiston, Australia: The Edwin Mellen Press, 2003.

Meyer, Milton W. *China: A Concise History,* 2nd ed., rev. Lanham, Md.: Rowman & Littlefield Publishers, Inc., 1994.

Milnor, Seaver Johnson. "A Comparison between the Development of the Chinese Writing System and Dongba Pictographs." In *University of Washington Working Papers in Linguistics,* vol. 24, edited by Daniel J. Jinguji and Steven Moran, 30–45. Seattle: Linguistics Department, University of Washington, 2005.

Morrison, Robert. *A Dictionary of the Chinese Language.* Charleston, S.C.: Nabu Press, 2010. First published before 1923.

Pregadio, Fabrizio, ed. *The Routledge Encyclopedia of Taoism.* 2 vols. New York: Routledge, 2011.

Rock, Joseph Francis Charles. *The Ancient Na-Khi Kingdom of Southwest China.* Cambridge, Mass.: Harvard University Press, 1947.

———. *A Na-Khi–English Encyclopedic Dictionary,* part I. Rome: Istituto Italiano Per Il Medio Ed Estremo Oriente, 1963.

Rosemont, Henry, Jr. *Explorations in Early Chinese Cosmology.* Chico, Calif.: Scholars Press, 2006.

Scranton, Laird. *The Cosmological Origins of Myth and Symbol: From the Dogon and Ancient Egypt to India, Tibet, and China.* Rochester, Vt.: Inner Traditions, 2010.

———. *Sacred Symbols of the Dogon: The Key to Advanced Science in the Ancient Egyptian Hieroglyphs.* Rochester, Vt.: Inner Traditions, 2007.

———. *The Science of the Dogon: A Study of the Founding Symbols of Civilization.* Rochester, Vt.: Inner Traditions, 2006.

Smith, Richard. *Fathoming the Cosmos and Ordering the World: The Yijing (I-Ching, or Classic of Changes) and Its Evolution in China.* Charlottesville: University of Virginia Press, 1999.

Snodgrass, Adrian. *Architecture, Time, and Eternity.* Delhi, India: Aditya Prakashan, 1990.

———. *The Symbolism of the Stupa.* Delhi, India: Motilal Banarsidass Publishers, 1992.

Wheatley, Paul. *The Pivot of the Four Quarters: A Preliminary Enquiry into the Origins and Character of the Ancient Chinese City.* Chicago: Aldine Publishing Company, 1971.

Xiaoping, Ji. *Worshiping the Three Sage Kings and Five Virtuous Emperors.* Beijing, China: Foreign Languages Press, 2007.

Xu, Zhentao, David W. Pankenier, and Yaotiao Jiang. *East Asian Archeoastronomy: Historical Records of Ancient Observations of China, Japan, and Korea.* Amsterdam, the Netherlands: Gordon and Breach Science Publisher, 2000.

INDEX

BOOKS OF RELATED INTEREST

Point of Origin
Gobekli Tepe and the Spiritual Matrix for the World's Cosmologies
by Laird Scranton

The Cosmological Origins of Myth and Symbol
From the Dogon and Ancient Egypt to India, Tibet, and China
by Laird Scranton

The Science of the Dogon
Decoding the African Mystery Tradition
by Laird Scranton

Sacred Symbols of the Dogon
The Key to Advanced Science in the Ancient Egyptian Hieroglyphs
by Laird Scranton

The Velikovsky Heresies
Worlds in Collision and Ancient Catastrophes Revisited
by Laird Scranton

The Sacred Science of Ancient Japan
Lost Chronicles of the Age of the Gods
by Avery Morrow

Forgotten Civilization
The Role of Solar Outbursts in Our Past and Future
by Robert M. Schoch, Ph.D.

Gobekli Tepe: Genesis of the Gods
The Temple of the Watchers and the Discovery of Eden
by Andrew Collins

INNER TRADITIONS • BEAR & COMPANY
P.O. Box 388
Rochester, VT 05767
1-800-246-8648
www.InnerTraditions.com

Or contact your local bookseller